D1480424

16PF®

INTERPRETATION IN CLINICAL PRACTICE:

A Guide to the Fifth Edition

Michael Karson, Ph.D., A.B.P.P., Clinical

Samuel Karson, Ph.D., A.B.P.P., Clinical

Jerry O'Dell, Ph.D.

Institute for Personality and Ability Testing, Inc.
P.O. Box 1188, Champaign, Illinois 61824-1188

IPAT

Since this book's publication in 1997, the publisher of the 16PF® Fifth Edition Questionnaire has released updated norms (January, 2002).

With the original norms, three primary personality factors were available with sex-specific norms – Warmth (A), Dominance (E), and Sensitivity (I). With the updated norms, Factors A (Warmth) and I (Sensitivity) can still be scored with sex-specific norms. In addition, Apprehension (O) now has sex-specific norms. However, sex-specific norms for Dominance (E) are no longer available.

Detailed information about the updated norms can be found in the *16PF Fifth Edition Norm Supplement, Release 2002*. To purchase this supplement, please call IPAT Customer Service at 1-800-225-4728.

The following copy reflects the above changes and replaces the first sentence of the first full paragraph on page 147 in *16PF*® Interpretation in Clinical Practice: A Guide to the Fifth Edition.

Three of the 16PF scales – Warmth (A), Sensitivity (I), and Apprehension (O) – can be scored with either combined-sex or sex-specific norms.

DEDICATION

For Dorothy Karson

TABLE OF CONTENTS

CHAPTER 5
RESPONSE SET OR VALIDITY SCALES

CHAPTER 6
GLOBAL FACTORS

CHAPTER 8
CASE STUDIES

Acknowledgments

We wish to thank Mary Russell and James Slaughter at IPAT for their many valuable comments at every stage of the project. Re-reading some of Professor Raymond Cattell's work in preparing this manuscript has reminded us how vigorous and insightful his thinking has been for over half a century, and we are indebted to him. We would like to thank our copy editor, Judy O'Donnell, who has improved virtually every paragraph.

Originally, this book was to have been a revision of Karson & O'Dell's 1976 book, updating it for the 16PF Fifth Edition, and to some extent it still is. To the extent that it is not, however, it owes a great deal to its predecessor. Sections on the development of the test, and on Factors G and O, have been taken whole from the previous work, in some cases with quotation marks and in others paraphrased. Permission from IPAT to use this material, as well as some tables and a graph from the administrator's manual, is gratefully acknowledged.

FOREWORD

This interpretive guide is well-organized, clearly written, and easy to use. The authors highlight the important red flags early in the book so that the clinician will be aware of the ways that 16PF scores might be related to the pathology. An interpretive strategy is provided which is logical and incremental in complexity. The importance of the validity scales; the use, value and complexity of the global factors; the interpretation of interaction between the primary factor scales; and the relevance of obtained scores to the therapeutic relationship are explained in easily understood language and illustrated by case example. The authors share their vast clinical experience as well as the research literature in explaining apparent contradictions in obtained scale scores. This is a practical guide that suggests therapeutic intervention based on profile interpretation. It is filled with case examples that illustrate how the treatment strategy was informed by test data and provide the reader with outcome information.

In this edition of the guide, case examples reflect current client problems and practice trends. There are many more cases in which relationship issues are prominent and systemic issues are addressed, sometimes in a couples' or family therapy modality. There is frequent recognition of the larger social context, in particular the effects of gender socialization on personality traits and male/female relationships. The cases themselves are indicative of contemporary problems, such as custody issues, juvenile delinquency and the changing roles of women and men in today's society. Many cases are discussed in terms of object relations theory, while others illustrate brief strategic methods of treatment, both of which reflect current trends in practice. This guide is clearly clinically relevant to topics in contemporary practice.

Several years ago I had the privilege of serving on the clinical faculty of the School of Psychology of Florida Tech with Sam Karson, co-author of the 1976 edition of this book. At the time, Sam lamented that the students no longer understood his "famous" examples of primary factor scales. Greta Garbo? Mae West? Errol Flynn? Who were these people? He asked me to help him think of contemporary examples which might be more recognizable to today's students. In effect, *16PF Interpretation in Clinical Practice: A Guide to the Fifth Edition* has done just that for today's clinicians. In addition to incorporating the vast knowledge gained through twenty more years of experience in using the 16PF in clinical practice, this volume places the 16PF in the context of the present—in terms of the sociological arena as well as the realities of contemporary clinical practice. It is a valuable contribution to the assessment literature and an indispensable tool for the practicing clinician.

Carol L. Philpot, Psy.D.
Professor Emeritus, Florida Institute of Technology

Reference

Szasz, T. (1974). *The myth of mental illness.* New York: Harper & Row.

CHAPTER 1
THE CLINICAL RELEVANCE OF THE 16PF

The 16PF, unlike many psychological tests used in clinical practice, was not developed to solve a clinical problem. For example, its aim was never to categorize patients, to identify retarded children or schizophrenics, nor to expose psychological conflicts for therapeutic intervention. Instead, the 16PF was created in the laboratory to measure personality itself. Because of its unique origin and purpose, the 16PF is an instrument that integrates two domains having a long history of division: the experimental exploration of personality structure versus the instruments and techniques favored by clinicians.

According to one interpretation of the history of psychology (and of medicine), clinicians repeatedly used makeshift instruments and techniques because they could not wait for scientific inquiry to shed its slow light on clinical problems. These instruments and techniques were improved or discarded in the evolutionary marketplace of ideas according to how well they seemed to work. Unfortunately, the associated theory was often spurious (Skinner, 1953, p. 30), reducing its ability to produce useful innovations. Meanwhile, science made its own progress, independent of the need to help specific clients and under the rules of a different marketplace in which experimental effects were weighed more heavily than immediate therapeutic benefits. For a long time, clinicians regarded such scientific inquiry as naive about the complexity of psychological problems. Early efforts to transpose the behaviorism of the laboratory to the clinical setting were barely referenced by leading clinicians. For example, Freud made only one trivial reference in his complete works to Pavlov and none at all to Thorndike or Watson. Presumably, Freud ignored these scientists—even though they were laying the groundwork for understanding contemporary behaviorism—because he believed their work had little to say about immediate clinical concerns.

Cattell (1976, p. ix) addressed these issues in his foreword to Karson & O'Dell's *A Guide to the Clinical Use of the 16PF:*
> Until quite recent times, the factor-analytic,
> experimental exploration of personality structure
> on the one hand, and the conceptions and
> measurements used by clinicians on the other,
> have grown up in two domains with an iron
> curtain between them. Yet anyone versed in
> the history of science would realize that since
> they were converging by different methods upon
> the same concepts, the practitioners and the
> researchers must sooner or later get together.

Recognition of the clinical relevance of the 16PF is growing. In comparing the 16PF with the MMPI, Golden (1990) noted:
> The 16PF was not originally designed as a clinical
> instrument, and has seen little clinical use and
> research compared with the MMPI. There is
> an impressive amount of research literature on
> the 16PF, but it does not generally address the
> medical and psychiatric problems seen by
> many clinical psychologists. This state of affairs
> has begun to change in recent years, however
> (Krug, 1977; Cattell, H.B., 1989; Meyer, 1993).
> . . . [Clinical research with the 16PF] is appearing
> in such publications as the *Journal of Consulting
> and Clinical Psychology* and the *Journal of
> Personality Assessment.* This growing literature,
> aimed at the clinician rather than the experimen-
> tal personality theorist, indicates a valid and
> growing use for the 16PF in clinical practice.

A study (Watkins, Campbell, Nieberding, & Hallmark, 1995) on the frequency of use of assessment procedures by clinical psychologists also supports this trend. In fact, the escalating demand for the 16PF as a tool in psychotherapy can be traced to several factors: (1) the need to adapt therapeutic services to the economic realities of managed care; (2) the need to accommodate increasing requests for therapeutic services by the "normal" population; (3) an enhanced appreciation for the relevance of ordinary personality traits in diagnosing clinical problems; and (4) recognition of the 16PF's capability to facilitate a therapeutic dialogue between the clinician and client.

THE IMPACT OF MANAGED CARE

Major trends in psychotherapy practice ensure the continued relevance of the 16PF to clinical work. One such trend is the increased likelihood that under managed care systems, therapists will have to justify, document the effectiveness of, and limit their services. Thus, beyond use in the therapy encounter itself, objective personality tests such as the 16PF can assist the clinician in demonstrating the presence of a problem that is susceptible to therapeutic intervention. In justifying treatments to third-party payers, post-treatment testing also may become widespread as quality assurance and cost-saving dynamics require clinicians to document the effectiveness of their techniques. Primarily, though, the impact of managed care on the usefulness of the 16PF in clinical practice relates to the need to reduce expensive client contact hours, such as those used in assessment interviews for therapies.

Whether even extended assessments of therapy clients by clinical interview can compete with psychological testing to produce reliable and valid information is questionable (Kleinmutz, 1982). However, therapists have long preferred to gather information via clinical interview rather than testing for a variety of reasons. The clinical interview allows the client to control, or more accurately, to feel in control of the information presented. Assessment by clinical interview also feels more "natural" than testing to many clients, especially those concerned about being dehumanized. Conducting assessments for therapies by interview promotes a smooth integration of assessment and treatment; that is, the information can be discussed as it is obtained. Even more importantly, an alliance between therapist and client can be developed around the acquisition of information when assessment is conducted by interview, and this alliance usually carries over into therapeutic tasks. Such a working alliance also enhances the creation of a meaningful narrative to make sense of the data. Clinical interview is viewed as better than testing for promoting emotional bonds between therapist and client. It enables the therapist to make each new inquiry relevant to the topic of discussion, thus

capitalizing on the client's desire for help as a motivator for providing good information. In contrast, testing involves asking the
same questions of every client in the same order, and the questions' apparent lack of relevance to the client's particular problem
can diminish motivation to answer them fully and honestly.

Under managed care, the previously cited advantages of clinical
interviews over psychological testing become largely moot. A
therapist simply does not have the time to develop a mutual
understanding of the presenting problem, its underlying conflicts,
and the client's identity at the client's own pace. Instead, the
therapist must conform to brief treatment demands largely by
addressing only the presenting symptom or by squeezing every
client into a favorite Procrustean bed, regardless of how well it
fits. Consequently, ready-made treatment strategies, always a
recourse for therapists unable to tailor their understanding of a
person or situation to the unique features, are becoming epidemic
under managed care.

With the aid of the 16PF, therapists do not have to ignore a
client's larger personality in designing a symptom-oriented treatment plan, nor must they assume that the client's personality is
suitable for a ready-made treatment plan. Instead, they can
administer the 16PF to assess their client's actual personality functioning rather than ignore it or make assumptions. This enables
treatment planning to unfold in a context that takes the client's
individual personality into account. Administration of the 16PF
can be considered analogous to the medical practice of gathering
systemic data (weight, blood pressure, heart rate, etc.) on a
patient, regardless of the presenting problem, to guard against the
possibility that a simple symptom is hiding a systemic disease.
The 16PF information can be shared in a therapeutic dialogue
with the client. Bringing the test results into treatment preserves
many of the advantages of obtaining information by clinical interview. Moreover, if the need for testing and the possible relevance
of its findings are explained beforehand to clients, they tend to
view the testing process as a positive experience.

From a managed-care perspective, the 16PF is a cheap source of
information since its administration does not require the clinician's presence (except perhaps in the logistics of a small private
practice). Typically, the test's directions can be reviewed with the

client by the clinician or by a trained clerical person, who can then leave while the client completes the 16PF independently. One way to successfully integrate the 16PF with brief treatment involves testing the client at the conclusion of the first session, with the understanding that the purpose is to help contextualize the presenting complaint by exploring the rest of the client's personality. The second session can include a discussion of the test results and their implications for identifying other foci for treatment or for clarifying the meaning of the original problem.

THE IMPACT OF SERVICE ACCESSIBILITY

A second trend in psychotherapy practice that enhances the utility of the 16PF is the extension of mental health services to so many people. The line between the client population and the normal population is disappearing rapidly. In contemporary American society, hardly anyone has not been in some kind of therapy due to the plethora of accessible programs and services: HMOs, EAPs, school adjustment counseling, substance abuse services, parent training for divorcing couples, psychotropic medication prescriptions by general practitioners, psychological treatments for a panoply of normal behaviors (e.g., dieting, smoking, grieving, and job seeking), college counseling, and counseling for every conceivable life transition. The implication for the 16PF is that as a test of normal personality, it now has an indisputable place in clinical practice because of the overlap between the client population and the general public.

THE RELEVANCE OF ORDINARY PERSONALITY TRAITS TO CLINICAL PROBLEMS

The 16PF measures personality traits found in the general population; however, even clients with diagnosable disturbances often can be usefully assessed with the 16PF. This is because many, though obviously not all, psychological problems are based on ordinary personality traits. For example, a mismatch between a normal personality trait and a person's situation, family member, roommate, or colleague could lead to trouble. Consider a highly sociable person working as a bank teller who expends too much time and attention on customers and not enough on transactions. Eventually, the stress that results from an escalating workload could lead to a counseling referral for the symptom produced by the stress (e.g., absenteeism). Another hypothetical case involves a lively and enthusiastic teenage girl who argues constantly with her orderly and compulsive father. These ordinary traits can produce clinically significant or undesirable family patterns.

A second category of psychological problems based on ordinary personality traits concerns conflicts within an individual. A woman who is shy but also outspoken and stubborn gets into repeated heated exchanges with colleagues that cause her to lose sleep. A man who is socially bold but emotionally reserved irritates others because he initiates relationships but then fails to maintain them through the necessary level of social contact. Because of the accessibility of psychotherapy and counseling, a professional might be consulted about the woman's sleepless nights and the man's demanding friends. In both situations, a test of ordinary personality functioning would be a useful diagnostic tool.

A third category includes ordinary traits that are expressed in excess. Not all excess is pathological (and not all pathology is excessive), but much of it is. Many of the problems that bring people into a therapist's office stem from extreme degrees of ordinary traits; however, this is not to imply that all pathological conditions can be construed merely as extreme expressions of everyday traits. Borderline rage is different from being very angry; schizoid withdrawal is different from being very reserved; and paranoid projection is different from being very suspicious (Kernberg, 1975). Yet on a measure of ordinary anger or emotional reservation or suspiciousness, the borderline, schizoid, or paranoid client probably would respectively receive an extreme score. Furthermore, even for those traits for which an extreme score does not suggest a primitive personality organization, the extremity alone could be theorized as the source of problems. For example, no pathology per se is implied by a heightened degree of assertiveness. Indeed, many formulations of mental health would label very assertive people as the healthiest (Nietzsche, 1886), and yet they are likely to experience problems just because they are so assertive. The same can be true for excessive friendliness, liveliness, and sensitivity, among other traits. The point is that whether excessive trait expression is pathological or merely creates challenges, the clinician may be able to shed some valuable light on a client's complaints by identifying extreme personality traits and their implied behavior potentials. (See p. 18 for a list of 16PF extreme scores that indicate possible psychopathological conditions.)

ASSESSMENT HYGIENE

We think (with some forensic exceptions) that the results of an assessment should benefit the person assessed. Instruments with scales named after psychiatric disorders often complicate the clinicians' desire to make the assessment process therapeutic. Many simply do not provide client feedback from tests like the MMPI because the scales are difficult to discuss in neutral or vernacular terms. When clinicians do try to share MMPI results with clients in an effort to integrate and redeem the testing experience, a lot of uncomfortable mumbling is often heard. Consequently, the therapeutic alliance is undermined since the client's communication via the test's questions has disappeared into a void.

In contrast, information concerning nearly all of the 16PF scales can be discussed openly and easily with clients, thus enabling them to become full partners in the assessment process and subsequent therapy. The role that such a discussion offers clients may not be entirely in line with some kinds of therapy, specifically with treatments such as psychoanalysis and hypnosis that capitalize on, rather than diminish, the hierarchy in the dyad; however, many of the brief treatments occasioned by managed care— not to mention humanist, feminist, and consumeristic concerns about the power differential in therapy—thrive on a "democratic" working alliance. In fact, our experience indicates that therapists usually find 16PF results easier to share than their clinical impressions.

CHAPTER 2
GENERAL INTERPRETIVE CONSIDERATIONS

Note: Because our targeted reader is the practicing clinician, we consistently refer to 4 of the 16 primary factor scales by names that have greater clinical significance than their 16PF Fifth Edition names. Thus, we use Ego Strength (C), Assertiveness (E), Impracticality (M), and Compulsivity (Q3) instead of the Fifth Edition's Emotional Stability (C), Dominance (E), Abstractedness (M), and Perfectionism (Q3). Chapter 4 presents the history of the scales' names and a further explanation of our preferences.

AN ASSESSMENT IS A CONSULTATION

The interpretation of a 16PF profile does not proceed in a vacuum. It is informed by the referral question, the circumstances of the testing, and the client's characteristics. The interpretive report does not necessarily provide a comprehensive portrait of the client's personality; it answers a referral question (although sometimes the portrait is the referral question). The report is about a specific issue in a specific context.

The approach to a given client's 16PF profile can change markedly from one context to another. "This man came for therapy because his wife said she'd leave him if he didn't" creates a far different orientation toward a profile than "This cop was suspended for beating a suspect, but he wants to keep his target pistols." The first referral issue would lead to an immediate inspection of the profile. In contrast, the second referral issue would initially prompt questions about the beating, its aftermath, the officer's psychosocial adjustment, and why he believes retaining the pistols is justifiable. If the latter explanation is reasonable (e.g., he is convinced he will be exonerated and wants to maintain his target practice routine), the psychologist might not concur with it but probably would proceed to examine the 16PF profile. If the explanation is ominous (e.g., having the pistols and not needing them is preferable to needing them and not having them), the psychologist would have to conclude that nothing in the client's 16PF profile could possibly produce a recommendation to keep the pistols.

Determining which test or tests to administer depends on the referral question. Obviously, the main premise for this book is to explain how the 16PF can play an active role in answering many clinical questions. Such questions do not always require testing, but when they do, the 16PF usually can offer substantial feedback. In our opinion, referral questions that are unlikely to be answered via 16PF results mainly concern issues such as psychosis and inpatient treatment. This is because certain groups of people may not express themselves accurately on the 16PF, either because they do not resemble the norm sample or because the testing situation or the test items are foreign to their experience. For example, we do not recommend administering the 16PF to chronic welfare recipients or chronic mental patients.

Blind interpretations, in which the psychologist responds only to the test data and perhaps also to age and sex, generally contradict our view of assessment as a consultation. Sometimes, an expert may be asked to conduct a blind interpretation on the results of a specific test when, and only when, his or her remarks are to be integrated into a comprehensive interpretation. In these situations, the expert plays the same role as the psychologist who approaches each new bit of data, or each test in the battery, with a fresh and open attitude. Indeed, when clinicians test their own patients, they must play all three roles: expert, consultant, and consultee. Although computerized test interpretations can be useful as blind-interpretation tools, they require a clinician's expertise to integrate them with other available information and to develop an answer to the referral question. Suggestions for approaching a 16PF profile, then, must be understood as analogous to a blind interpretation. Certainly most clinical questions that a psychologist tries to answer with the 16PF will demand an understanding of the client's test-taking attitude and will benefit from an effort to estimate the client's overall adjustment. However, no programmed approach to profile interpretation can consider all the relevant issues, so our suggestions should be viewed only as a starting point.

MEASUREMENT MAKES THINGS OBVIOUS

We measure something when we cannot discern what we want to know about it just by looking at it. For example, we may be able to know just by looking at a certain sofa whether it would fit along a stretch of wall. If we cannot tell by looking, then we would have to measure. We would hold a tape measure against both the sofa and wall, and the markings on the tape would make it obvious whether the sofa would fit along the wall. If, instead of a sofa, we were interested in fitting a lens into a periscope, we would require a much more precise "yardstick" before it became obvious whether the lens would fit.

Likewise, sometimes what we want to know about people is obvious, and sometimes it is not. For example, a client sitting quietly in the waiting area of a college counseling center was so obviously having a psychotic episode that arrangements for his hospitalization were initiated before the therapist even introduced himself. A senior clinician reported that the client's eyes looked like the concentric circles used by cartoonists to depict insanity. Another example involves a father who had knocked out his son while moving furniture. The man was so devastated, remorseful, and yet able to see the humor in the situation (once his son was pronounced all right) that it was obvious to hospital personnel that involving the child welfare agency was unnecessary.

Not all clinical questions are as obvious as those in the preceding examples. Psychological testing is done because by having a client respond to standardized stimuli, much more can be learned than by interview. Consider that a sten score of 1 on Warmth (A) can make obvious what on interview seemed only an impression. In fact, all psychometric statistics, like measurements, are used in the service of making things obvious, whether the statistics represent a deviance on a certain trait or a high percentage of Rorschach responses involving animals. (Statistics also can be used to disprove what seems obvious, as in the case of differences between scores. All too often, clinicians think two scores are obviously different until the standard error of measurement demonstrates the contrary.) In developing the 16PF, Cattell (1946) used very complicated statistics to try to make obvious what factors underlie our descriptions of ourselves and others.

SOURCES OF INFLUENCE ON A STEN SCORE

Trait scores on the 16PF are affected by three major sources of influence, all of which relate in one way or another to the actual trait. All three need to be considered in interpreting a profile. First, some variance stems from declarations on the part of clients, which amount to communications to the tester or the referral source about where they belong on a given scale. Next, some variance stems from clients' characterizations of themselves, or their expression of a self-concept. Such characterizations are not specifically geared toward communicating with the tester but are enduring self-representations. Finally, some variance stems from measurement of the trait, or how clients acknowledge examples of the trait in relatively subtle or difficult-to-fake items.

DECLARATIONS

Declarations, or communications to the tester, are likely to reflect an actual trait accurately when clients have self-knowledge of the trait and are motivated to share that knowledge honestly. For example, most people can represent how shy they are, and unless a sales job is their objective, will freely do so. In contrast, most people cannot explain how much ego strength they have, and probably would decline to do so even if they could.

The 16PF is structured in such a way, and most of its items are obvious enough, that extreme scores usually involve some degree of communication on the part of clients. In addition to (probably) being extremely submissive, individuals who score very low on Assertiveness (E) are declaring the extent of their submissiveness. The scales most susceptible to reflecting the communicative intent of clients are those with the most obvious and the most repetitive items. Thus, scores on Ego Strength (C), Assertiveness (E), Liveliness (F), Rule-Consciousness (G), Social Boldness (H), Vigilance (L), Impracticality (M), Apprehension (O), and Tension (Q4) are likely to reflect the communicative intent of clients. This does not invalidate these scores as measures of the traits, but it does add a complicating consideration. When interpreting the scores, the clinician must consider not only how the client manages the traits but also why the client wants the clinician to think of him or her in a certain way.

Psychological tests and interviews interface with different aspects of the client. Interviews are mediated by the client's social persona, whereas different psychological tests are mediated by other parts of the client's self. Thus, in contrast to interviews, testing enables the gathering of more information and approaching the client through more varied avenues. For example, a client may represent herself during an interview as having a lot of friends, whereas her testing results may represent her as aloof, shy, and self-reliant. To understand the client's two different self-representations, consideration needs to be given as to how the interview situation differs from the testing experience for her. Often, the testing experience occasions a reflective aspect of the person, while the interview may stimulate authority, sexual, or competitive issues. To some people, the interview seems social and the testing, impersonal and authoritarian.

CHARACTERIZATIONS

The entire 16PF profile can be seen as a reflection of identity. Aspects of the self hidden from awareness are likely to be hidden from the 16PF, while acknowledged aspects of the self are likely to be reflected in profile scores. This is because the 16PF focuses not only on normal traits but also on surface traits. The test is particularly strong in predicting public behavior; that is, where the same persona is manifested that is activated by the test questions. Tests such as the Rorschach or Early Memories, which activate internal resources in responding to the test stimuli, provide a better glimpse of a client's inner life than does the 16PF. (Indeed, the 16PF and the Rorschach comprise an excellent tandem for addressing most clinical questions, although administering and interpreting the Rorschach is time consuming.)

Thus, the 16PF profile needs to be examined not only as an assessment of trait strengths but also as an expression of self-concept. This is a crucial aspect of personality assessment that should not be minimized, for people's self-concepts may be more important than their actual trait strengths in determining how they will behave. For example, a schizoid man from a schizoid family came to define himself as sociable because he was the only member of his family who could actually hold a conversation that did not concern work. He avoided people as much as any schizoid person, but when thrust into social encounters, he behaved in an urbane, self-confident, and engaging manner. (It took a long time for his therapist, who did not give him the 16PF, to determine that their apparent relationship was a charade.) This man was urbane because he believed he was urbane.

To be oneself may be the ultimate human personality motive. This motive is not easily recognized because it is so ubiquitous. Since most people seek only situations that reflect and reinforce their self-concept, they typically are embedded in a made-to-order psychosocial environment. The expression of need for a comfortable environment is analogous to that for oxygen; only when people are deprived of oxygen is their interest in it manifested, and only when people are thrust into a situation where they cannot be themselves do they struggle to do so. Therefore, a self-report inventory that reveals what people consider to be their self-concept is in many ways as important for the clinician as a more subtle effort to measure personality traits that bypass the self-concept. In fact, it is useful to formulate impressions of some scale scores by prefixing them with the phrase, "Someone who scored the way this person did. . . ." Often, it is not the personality trait that will not allow certain behaviors, but the person who claims to have the trait who will not.

MEASUREMENT

No matter how badly clients want to appear intelligent, they will not score high on Factor B (Reasoning) if they cannot figure out the scale's problems. No other factor reaches this level of independence from clients' interests in communicating or in expressing self-concept, although all have items that are not consciously influenced because they are subtle or because either response is socially acceptable. Sensitivity (I) and Openness to Change (Q1) are especially immune to motivational distortions and self-expressions, but every sten score is influenced to some extent by the degree to which clients express or possess the trait in question. This influence on sten scores is what is traditionally considered construct validity.

PROFILE INTERPRETATION IS A PROCESS

The following steps comprise our recommended basic strategy for interpreting a 16PF profile.

Step 1: Evaluate Test-taking Attitude

The validity or response-style scales, which attempt to measure motivational distortion or random responding, usually do not contribute much useful information to the profile interpretation; however, when they do, processing them first is crucial. They may indicate that the profile is too invalid to warrant further examination. More typically, the profile data cannot be validly understood apart from the information regarding how it was produced. Thus, the clinician should always examine Impression Management (IM), Acquiescence (ACQ), and Infrequency (INF) before proceeding with the profile interpretation. (See chapter 5 also.)

Step 2: Evaluate Overall Adjustment

Naturally, clinicians are interested in assessing neurosis in its broadest sense (e.g., psychopathology, neuroticism, unresolved conflict, psychic inefficiency, disadvantageous functioning, and inflexibility) as well as the opposite—overall mental health, emotional stability, personality integration, and adjustment. Many nonclinicians seem to consider neuroticism a dichotomous variable, as if people are either in the "clinical range" or not. We think of it as a continuous—though not necessarily as a normally distributed—variable that can usefully describe the following at all levels: adjustment potential, psychological resources, adaptability, and frustration tolerance. A medical analogy would be the measurement of heart rate and blood pressure, by which physicians acquire meaningful data even in the "subclinical" range.

Overall adjustment is of interest to clinicians not only because related problems are what they are typically hired to address but also because an accurate understanding of many behaviors depends on first understanding the overall psycho-developmental context. Jacobson (1971) clarifies the role of overall psychopathology in understanding depression in particular, showing how the concept of depression varies tremendously according to a client's overall adjustment. Kernberg's (1975, 1984) work depends heavily on the concept of levels of mental health; he uses the examples of femininity, hysterical personality, infantile personality, and hebephrenia to show the importance of levels of pathology in determining how a set of traits will be expressed.

On the 16PF, the impression of overall adjustment stems from four main sources:
1. The score on Ego Strength (C) influences all other interpretive efforts.
2. The score on Anxiety (AX) provides the best indicator of current emotional adjustment and overall symptomatology.
3. Scores on Compulsivity (Q3) and Self-Control (SC) can indicate compensating strengths when ego deficiencies are evident elsewhere.
4. The number of scores that raise questions about adjustment ("areas to explore") can be seen as representing the likelihood of finding the person operating in a sphere of problematic functioning.

Problem scores on the 16PF Fifth Edition are extreme scores that indicate the following traits:[1]

Social Withdrawal.* Very low scores on Warmth (A) suggest an avoidance of other people that goes beyond a preference for being alone. Problems in forming and maintaining interpersonal relationships are likely, as is a history of unsatisfying transactions with others.

Poor Reasoning Ability. Although not in and of itself an indicator of psychopathology, a very low score on Reasoning (B) may indicate that major conflicts are impairing the individual's intellectual functioning. Furthermore, true deficits in verbal facility increase the likelihood that other personality problems will be unmodulated.

---

*Above-average scores on a given factor are referred to by a plus sign (+), and low scores, by a minus sign (-), thus yielding A-, E+, AX+, and so forth.

Low Ego Strength. Very low scores on Ego Strength (C) suggest severe coping deficits, poor frustration tolerance, and difficulty in deferring needs when required.

Submissiveness. Extremely low scores on Assertiveness (E) suggest problems involving the smooth integration of aggression with other psychological functions. This can lead to chronic resentment or to explosive episodes when aggression is inhibited over time.

Low Energy Level. Extremely low scores on Liveliness (F) suggest a depressed mood or other problems with enjoyment.

Unconventionality. Very low scores on Rule-Consciousness (G) suggest disenfranchisement from societal expectations of behavior.

Shyness. Extremely low scores on Social Boldness (H) indicate a social timidity and fear of others that may be based on self-esteem problems.

Suspiciousness. Extremely high scores on Vigilance (L) suggest problems with the projection of anger and a preoccupation with power dynamics.

Impracticality. Very high scores on Impracticality (M) may indicate a detachment from the mundane issues of life that is likely to interfere with the individual's competence and effectiveness.

Worrying. Very high scores on Apprehension (O) are probably associated with a negative self-experience, attacks of conscience, or a degree of apprehension that is likely to interfere with the person's functioning.

Aversion to Change. Extremely low scores on Openness to Change (Q1) suggest a severe constriction in response variability that impairs the individual's capacity to meet new demands flexibly.

Difficulty Collaborating. Extremely high scores on Self-Reliance (Q2) suggest conflicts with getting dependency needs met and with establishing and maintaining mutually gratifying relationships.

Disorderliness. Very low scores on Compulsivity (Q3) raise questions about the individual's identity integration, discipline, orderliness, sense of purpose, and self-esteem.

Tension. Very high scores on Tension (Q4) suggest a level of tension and anxiety that is likely to interfere with the person's functioning efficiency.

Poor Impression Management. Too little attribution of socially desirable behaviors to oneself can signal problems in self-esteem or adjustment problems that derive from insensitivity to social cues.

Step 3: Focus First on Extreme Scores

If measurement makes things obvious, then interpretation should focus on what stands out. The 16PF profile sheet contains no gripping metaphors, no rich narratives, and no turns of phrase to stop the clinician short. Instead, the clinician should be alert to extreme scores, which are scores greater than 7 or less than 4. Extreme scores are not as rare as might be supposed (Russell & Karol, 1994, p. 29 and p. 40).

TABLE 1

NUMBER OF EXTREME PRIMARY FACTOR SCORES
ON 16PF PROFILES (BASED ON NORM SAMPLE, $\underline{N}$=2500)

Number of Extremes	Percent of Sample	Cumulative Percent
0	1.0	1.0
1	4.5	5.5
2	8.6	14.1
3	13.4	27.5
4	15.4	42.9
5	15.1	58.0
6	14.4	72.4
7	10.5	82.9
8	7.7	90.6
9	5.0	95.6
10	2.5	98.1
11	1.0	99.1
12	0.5	99.6
13-15	0.4	100.0

Note. From "Profile Interpretation" by M. Russell and D. Karol, 1994.
In *The 16PF Fifth Edition Administrator's Manual.* Champaign, IL: IPAT

TABLE 2

NUMBER OF EXTREME GLOBAL FACTOR SCORES ON 16PF
PROFILES (BASED UPON NORM SAMPLE, N=2500)

Number of Extreme Scores	Percent of Sample	Cumulative Percent
0	26.4	26.4
1	29.5	55.9
2	22.7	78.6
3	15.1	93.8
4	5.0	98.7
5	1.3	100.0

Note. From "Profile Interpretation" by M. Russell and D. Karol, 1994. In *The 16PF Fifth Edition Administrator's Manual.* Champaign, IL: IPAT

Step 4: Relate Scores to Referral Question

The clinician should continually consider how each score may relate to the referral question or the problem at hand by following a line of inquiry such as the following:
1. Which scores suggest pathologically disadvantageous trends?
2. Which scores suggest conflict between the trait and circumstances? Does the profile fit the psychosocial history? How can discrepancies be explained?
3. Which scores conflict with each other? What does the rest of the profile suggest about ways in which the individual manages this conflict?

WRITING READABLE REPORTS

The following are some general principles on report writing, which we have developed during our years of teaching psychological testing to graduate students:
1. Avoid making tautological statements such as "She runs away because she has poor impulse control," "He gets into fights because he has problems with aggression," and "She shoplifts because she wants what she wants when she wants it."
2. A report should be no longer than the assessment on which it is based; that is, reading the report should take less time than that spent by the psychologist with the client. Our years of observing readers of psychological reports (including therapists, social

workers, school personnel, parents, and clients) confirm that, invariably, the reader immediately flips to the last two pages. Why not write a report that contains only the content of these two pages to ensure that the vital information is read?

3. Depending on the referral circumstances, reports can be designed to offer hypotheses for consideration or a professional opinion or both. Hypotheses should not be so cautious as to undermine their utility. Opinions should be stated clearly even though they necessarily must represent limitations on certainty.

4. While specificity is desirable, it should not exceed the bounds of credulity. No personality test can determine whether a specific behavior has occurred in the past. No personality test can reveal what a person does for fun, thinks of welfare reform, or eats for breakfast.

AN EXAMPLE OF A 16PF INTERPRETATION

A 6-year-old boy was referred for therapy after striking his first-grade teacher, a woman. As part of the intake process, the 16PF was administered to both parents. The consulting psychologist was asked to interpret the father's profile and to comment on its implications for the boy's treatment. The father was a carpenter in his late 20s.

THE FATHER'S 16PF SCORES

PRIMARY TRAIT SCORES

Factor		Sten
A	Warmth	3
B	Reasoning	4
C	Ego Strength	6
E	Assertiveness	8
F	Liveliness	3
G	Rule-Consciousness	6
H	Social Boldness	3
I	Sensitivity	1
L	Vigilance	10
M	Impracticality	5
N	Privateness	5
O	Apprehension	3
Q1	Openness to Change	6
Q2	Self-Reliance	8
Q3	Compulsivity	7
Q4	Tension	7

RESPONSE SET SCORES

Scale		Percentile
IM	Impression Management	15
ACQ	Acquiescence	65
INF	Infrequency	51

GLOBAL FACTOR SCORES

Scale		Sten
EX	Extraversion	2.9
AX	Anxiety	6.3
TM	Tough-Mindedness	8.2
IN	Independence	7.3
SC	Self-Control	7.0

PSYCHOLOGIST'S INTERPRETATION

This is an extremely suspicious man (L = 10) who identifies strongly with a traditional masculine ideal (I = 1). A paranoid adjustment has to be considered, especially in light of the psychoanalytic concept of paranoia as a defense against feelings of sex-role inadequacy. This man may be bolstering a sense of failure as a man by denying any traditionally feminine attributes, which he may see as weak, and by holding others responsible for his failures.

Judging from his marked introversion (EX = 2.9), he is apparently a loner. He is basically uncomfortable with people; for example, he is reserved (A = 3), constrained (F = 3), shy (H = 3), and solitary (Q2 = 8). Because he tends to avoid people, he is unlikely to have a social network that could balance his sense of inadequacy by making him feel appreciated. His low score on Impression Management reinforces this hypothesis since it may signal a disregard for the opinions of others. His lack of social skills may produce a vicious circle of being an outcast and then responding with anger and feelings of inadequacy that further distance him from others. This may lead him to focus his self-esteem issues on the few relationships he does maintain, especially those with his wife and child. He may expect to have more control over them (SC = 7.0, E = 8) than is realistic, and then may interpret his lack of control as further evidence of his deteriorating manhood.

His orderliness (Q3 = 7), emotional stability (C = 6), and conventionality (G = 6) indicate a capacity to present well when his self-esteem issues are not activated, which may put him at his best while he is at work. Indeed, work may soothe his self-questioning by making him feel that he is discharging his masculine responsibilities. Under the surface, however, he is very aggressive (L = 10, E = 8, IN = 7.3). Further, his low score on Apprehension (O = 3) raises questions about the extent to which his conventional presentation is based on a genuine internalization of social norms versus a more expedient effort to stay out of trouble; in other words, some people who worry as little as he does are not as conscientious as they may appear.

His son has shown that he operates in a world in which striking a female in an authority role is the thing to do on occasion. The father's 16PF profile suggests that the boy's world may have been informed by psychological patterns that include compensating for feelings of inadequacy by identifying them as weak and feminine and blaming and intimidating others as a way of demonstrating mastery over frailty. Whether or not this man physically beats his wife, the child's individual therapy is not likely to progress very far if the weeks between sessions are spent in an environment where it would be frightening not to identify with the aggressor role. The parents' relationship needs to be investigated to ensure that the child is not being exposed to violence. In any case, the son's vision of masculine aggression is more likely to change if his father's does too.

CHAPTER 3
THE CONSTRUCTION OF THE 16PF

We do not intend to examine the construction of the 16PF in great depth, but do want to review its basic insight, which we regard as one of the best in psychology. Cattell's (1943) major purpose in constructing the 16PF was to provide an instrument that would measure the most fundamental dimensions of normal personality and comprehensively span the entire range of personality characteristics. His initial challenge concerned finding a set of descriptive categories sufficiently wide to encompass the many variations of human personality.

Cattell (1943) recognized that if a way of describing another person were useful, a word for it would exist, specifically an English-language adjective. Thus, Cattell began constructing his test by seeking adjectives that describe people instead of using the categories of clinical psychiatrists (which is where the MMPI began). The work of Allport and Odbert (1936) helped simplify Cattell's search. Allport and Odbert had combed the dictionary to compile a list of about 18,000 adjectives that could be used to describe human personality. The dictionary's entries may not represent a compilation of all the mysterious or technical concepts about people, but practically speaking, concepts that have not officially entered the language would be useless in describing most people's personalities.

Cattell thus proposed to use the personality-descriptive adjectives as the starting place for his test; however, developing a test that provided thousands of scores on an equal number of traits was neither practical nor desirable. Therefore, his goal became to reduce the thousands of adjectives to an optimal set of categories that retained as much information as possible from the list. By the 1940s, when Cattell was working to resolve this problem, a technique called *factor analysis* had been fairly well established by Spearman and others. Broadly speaking, factor analysis is a technique with a very simple purpose, which is to identify an optimal set of the fewest categories that retains the most information or accounts for the most variance. Variance, in respect to the development of the 16PF, is the quantification of the fact that people vary in how adjectives are applied to them by others. If all the adjectives meant the same thing or if everyone were described by others in the same way, no variance would exist.

The number of categories derived as a result of factor analysis is to some extent a judgment call. Indeed, Cattell is widely considered the "Father of the Big Five Personality Theory" (Goldberg, 1993), which holds that 5 factors can account for all the ways in which people vary.[1] In spite of his paternal appellation, Cattell (Cattell & Krug, 1986) believes that using only 5 factors loses too much information and instead maintains that 16 factors are required (the origin of the 16PF name).

The objective of factor analysis, then, is to discover how few and which factors are needed to account for the greatest amount of information. Some examples may help illustrate this process. The words *friendly, sociable,* and *extraverted* have different meanings, but the differences are so subtle that a single dimension or factor could be used to cover all three words and cause little information to be lost. This method of reducing categories is equivalent to eliminating synonyms. By contrast, *cold* and *shy* may seem too dissimilar to lump together under *introverted,* although Big Five theorists think that any information lost in doing so is compensated by the reduction in categories. Another way of reducing categories is to split words into two or more factors. Thus, no category is needed for *defiant* since its meaning is almost completely covered by a mixture of *resistant* and *aggressive.* Rating someone on *resistance* and on *aggression* but not on *defiance* would cause the loss of little information.

Cattell's problem of reducing thousands of descriptors to the basic underlying dimensions or factors of human personality would have been nicely alleviated by factor analysis except that in the 1940s, doing this procedure on even 100 variables was a sheer physical impossibility. The computations were extremely lengthy, repetitious, and boring. It was not uncommon for several people, working five days a week and eight hours a day, to spend about three years to handle 40 variables. Even then, the method used was only an approximation to the desired procedure. Thus to accelerate his research, Cattell also had to find other ways to reduce the number of adjectives. He basically used his own judgment to shorten the list to 171 categories (many of which were bipolar), and then used correlational techniques to pare these to 35 categories on which factor analysis was performed (see Cattell, 1973, for details of the process).

Cattell's analysis produced 12 to 15 factors that appeared to underlie the description of human personality in the English language. The factors were labeled alphabetically, A through O. Each factor emerged from the analysis as a set of numeric weights applied to the set of 35 categories. Interpretation of the nature of each factor began with an inspection of its corresponding weights and with naming it. Interpretation of the 16PF test begins with this theoretical understanding of the nature of the factor, but must be adjusted by clinical and research experience with the test itself to define what each scale actually measures. According to their alphabetic progression, the factors decrease somewhat in importance, or in their degree of accounting for how people describe people differently. Thus, Factor A (Warmth) is first in importance, Factor B (Reasoning) is second, Factor C (Ego Strength) is third, and so forth. Three of the 15 basic factors identified by Cattell—D, J, and K—were dropped eventually because based on other methods of evaluation, they did not prove to be very replicable in adults. Cattell initially required the factors to emerge in three formats: self-report questionnaires, ratings by others, and actual behavior observations.

The 3 English-language factors that were dropped were replaced by 4 factors appearing from other sources of data; these 4 were added to the 12 remaining factors, making 16 in all. Since the 4 factors originated only in studies based on self-report questionnaire data, they were distinguished from the other factors by being labeled Q1, Q2, Q3, and Q4 (Q is for questionnaire). These may be fully valid personality factors that, by their nature, are expressed better by self-report than by other people's descriptions. In using the 16PF clinically, no distinction is made between these scales and the others.

CHAPTER 4
THE SCALES OF THE 16PF

Interpretation of a test's scales begins with naming them. Sometimes the traits to be measured are specified before a test is constructed. These traits frequently are selected on the basis of theory (e.g., a test may be written to measure Murray's list of human needs) or on the basis of clinical usage (e.g., a test may focus on diagnostic categories).

The factor analysis that produced the 16PF was powerful because it did not specify any of the factors beforehand; it let the data speak for itself. Each factor emerged from the analysis as a set of weights on adjectives. The next step was to determine what the adjectives had in common and to name the factor accordingly. In some cases, Cattell created names for the traits since no single word or phrase seemed to do justice to the dimension that had emerged. As the test has evolved and as research and clinical practice have further clarified what the 16PF scales actually measure, some factors have been renamed. Although we refer to the majority of the factors by their Fifth Edition names in this guide, we advise readers to bear in mind that historically the factors have been labeled with letters. For example, the actual name of the first factor is "Factor A"; calling it "Warmth" is one interpretation of what constitutes "A-ness."[1]

SOURCES OF INTERPRETATION FOR THE SCALES

The nature of the primary and global (or second-order) factors is described in the *Handbook for the Sixteen Personality Factor Questionnaire* (Cattell, Eber, & Tatsuoka, 1970) and in Cattell's two other major works concerning the 16PF, *Personality and Motivation Structure and Measurement* (1957) and *Personality and Mood by Questionnaire* (1973). Our interpretations of efforts to measure the primary and global factors, as represented by Form A and the Fifth Edition, are based on several sources, the most important of which is our extensive clinical and research experience with the 16PF. In addition, we have incorporated the major clinical research literature on the 16PF, highlights of which are included in the bibliography.[2]

A word about the format of the 16PF scales is in order. All the scales (except Reasoning, Factor B) are treated as bipolar; in other words, they have two ends. This is in direct contrast to the scales of many personality tests in current use, which allow a client only to be high on a given trait. For example, most of the MMPI scales permit a client only to be hypochondriacal, depressive, or whatever. The status of low scores on MMPI scales is unclear. A distinct advantage of the 16PF is that there is virtually always something to comment on for each scale.

Scores on the 16PF scales are reported as "standard-ten" or "sten" scores, except for the scores on the Fifth Edition's test-taking attitude scales, which are reported as either raw scores or as percentiles (the format used in this guide). Stens are scores that have been adjusted so that for each scale, the mean is 5.5 and the standard deviation is 2. In general, primary sten scores are expressed by whole numbers. This is a good practice, since most personality tests, including the 16PF, cannot provide meaningful differentiations at more than 10 levels. Indeed, some psychologists group the scale scores into only 3 or 4 levels (e.g., low, average, and high), recognizing that the standard error of measurement for each scale makes the reporting of even a whole-number sten artificially precise. The problem with such large groupings is that a response to a single item can change a person's results too dramatically (e.g., from low to average). With the use of stens, a single item response can change a person's score on a given scale by a single point at most (e.g., from 3 to 4). The best policy is to keep in mind the standard error by thinking "around 3" (or "pretty low") when a score is 3.

In large samples, sten scores are distributed as described in Figure 1.

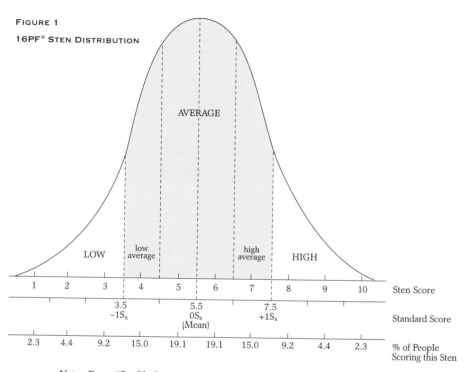

Note. From "Profile Interpretation" by M. Russell and D. Karol, 1994.
In *The 16PF Fifth Edition Administrator's Manual.* Champaign, IL: IPAT

Scores of 1 or 10 are each made by about 2.3% of people taking the 16PF; scores of 2 or 9, by about 4.4%; scores of 3 or 8, by about 9.2%; scores of 4 or 7, by about 15%; and scores of 5 or 6, by about 19.1%. Thus, the sten scale is normally distributed (and it is not the case that each of the 10 sten values is achieved by 10% of the population). On any given scale, most clients score about average, and extreme scores indicate extremes in the strength of the trait. A clinical interpretation should emphasize scores outside the 4-to-7 range, and most profiles provide a useful number of such scores (see Figure 1).

INTERPRETATIONS OF THE PRIMARY FACTOR SCALES

The discussion in this section, which is directed toward the clinical—or applied—user of the 16PF, concerns our hypotheses regarding the meanings of the 16PF primary factor scales. These hypotheses are based on our combined clinical and research experience with Form A and the Fifth Edition as well as on published studies. We consistently refer to the primary factors by their Fifth Edition names except for Factors C, E, M, and Q3, for which we use our preferred names. This is because our understanding of each of these factors differs significantly from what is implied by their Fifth Edition names. For each of the four factors, we introduce the Fifth Edition name (e.g., Emotional Stability [C]) followed by our preferred name in parentheses (e.g., Ego Strength [C]), and then continue to use our preference as we discuss the factor's meaning.

Although interactions between factors are mentioned in this section (e.g., possible meaning of a high score on Warmth [A+] when coupled with a low score on Social Boldness [H-]), they are not fully explored. Instead, they are discussed in depth in chapter 7.

We recommend that clinicians independently review each factor's test items so they can form their own a priori impressions of what the scales measure. To facilitate examining the items, we suggest physically cutting up a 16PF Fifth Edition test booklet so that the items can be arranged by scale. Otherwise, matching items with their scales involves alternating between Table 40 in *The 16PF Fifth Edition Administrator's Manual* (p. 134) and a test booklet.

Factor A: Warmth

Descriptors: Reserved, Impersonal, Distant (- pole) *versus* Warm, Outgoing, Attentive to Others (+ pole)

Factor A measures interpersonal warmth, sociability, and the desire to engage in emotional exchanges with others. People who score high on Warmth (A) move toward others and others tend to move toward them (Karson & O'Dell, 1989). An A+ person is a people person. This trait emerged first in the factor analysis, and is the main trait that people reference when describing others' personalities. Cattell (1957) notes that people high on Warmth (A) are probably "easygoing, adaptable (in habits), warmhearted, attentive to people, frank, emotional, expressive, trustful, impulsive, generous, and cooperative." High scorers want to be around people and are specifically interested in others' feelings.

Low scorers are inclined to prefer to be alone. Along with their reclusiveness, an emotional aloofness is often noted. They are less likely than high scorers to be concerned about how their actions and decisions may affect others. Thus, even though the scale's items ask mainly about emotions and socializing, inferences about objectivity versus intuitive subjectivity can be drawn. Indeed, "people persons" are often, but not always, less critical and less categorical as thinkers than are loners.

Extreme deviations on Warmth (A) can mean trouble, especially on the low end. Very low scorers not only prefer to be alone but also may have a schizoid tendency to withdraw from social contact. Typically, they move away from others and others move away from them. So many natural reinforcers (e.g., food, shelter, sex, and touch) are mediated by social transactions that, for most people, contact with others becomes secondarily reinforced in the process of growing up. Severe neglect or abuse, or a history of frustration or disappointment in relating to others, may induce the avoidance of social contact. Before inferring a pathological withdrawal from low scores, however, the clinician should check other indicators of mental health, including Ego Strength (C) and the Anxiety (AX) global factor. While very low scores on Warmth (A) are associated with poor performance in many jobs, some jobs such as bank teller attract so many people low on Warmth (A-) that the scale cannot be used to differentiate poor performers from good performers without considering other personality variables.[3]

Incidentally, Warmth (A) constitutes one of the main differences between good tellers and good customer service representatives. Even though the former interact with the public, they do so in a highly formalized, unengaged manner. On the other hand, customer service representatives specialize in relating to the public, anticipating and meeting their needs.

Extreme scores at the high end of Warmth (A) do not immediately signal the possibility of psychopathology, but may imply some problems. For example, the intensity of focus on other people suggests unmet dependency needs, as if each new face is searched for signs of gratification. This also could suggest a history of rewarding relationships with others, but at the extreme, the expectation would be of more satiation from rewarding relationships than very high scorers often experience. Instead, they frequently are perceived as "bottomless" in their need for social validation. Very high scorers can have trouble as supervisors or as parents because they cannot "set limits" or otherwise allow themselves to frustrate others. They sometimes prioritize other people's feelings above all other concerns. They also may have difficulty following through on paperwork, housework, or other tasks that do not involve interpersonal interactions.

Since most psychotherapies unfold in an interpersonal context, whether with the therapist or with family or group members, high scorers on Warmth (A) are often easy to engage in therapy. "Joining" techniques, in which the therapist establishes a relationship with the client to solidify a working alliance by developing emotional bonds, are likely to be effective with clients who score high on Warmth (A). Low scorers are unlikely to experience the therapy relationship as reason enough to engage in it and, indeed, may dislike the emphasis on feelings and relationships found in most therapies. A clear rationale that links discussion of these topics to the presenting complaint may be required.

Warmth (A) governs the extent to which relationships with other people are central to a person's identity definition and to his or her mode of interacting with the environment. High scorers tend to think of themselves as social beings, and may count their friendships as a way of feeling adequate. In most situations, the higher the score, the more likely other people's reactions turn out to be the relevant stimuli and the relevant consequences of high scorers' own actions. High scorers are typically considered by others to be good friends; extreme high scorers may even be renowned for their friendships and friendliness.

Four of the 11 items that measure Warmth (A) directly address emotions. This makes scoring high on Warmth (A) difficult if the client is actually high on the source trait but either lacks much interest in other people's feelings or dislikes admitting this interest (e.g., gregarious men who have been trained not to acknowledge an interest in emotions). Perhaps because of this, Warmth (A) is one of only three Fifth Edition scales that has separate norms for men and women.[4]

Factor B: Reasoning

Descriptors: Concrete (- pole) *versus* Abstract (+ pole)

Inclusion of this brief measure of one kind of intelligence in the 16PF represents a compromise between not measuring intellect at all (which is true of many personality tests) and devoting almost half the testing time to its measure (which occurs in many psychological evaluations). The scale's relevance is made clear by Cattell's (1950, p. 2) definition of personality as "that which permits a prediction of what a person will do in a given situation." Verbal puzzles were chosen in an effort to strike a balance between Cattell's concepts of crystallized and fluid intelligence, although as Cattell notes (1970, p. 82), the fact that the test is not timed makes it more of a "power" test than a "speed" test.

A Reasoning (B) score is affected by other variables besides the client's intellectual capacity in the verbal, problem-solving sphere. One obvious source of variance is the client's degree of familiarity with brainteasers or other forms of academic problem-solving. Families and subcultures expose members differently to these kinds of tasks and with varying degrees of seriousness. Scores can be artificially decreased by the novelty of the process of working out problems or artificially increased by its familiarity. Significant racial differences do exist on Reasoning (B) scores, with whites scoring higher than blacks. This is because blacks probably are, as a group, more poorly educated than whites (Conn & Rieke, 1994, pp. 27-29). When educational level is controlled for in the analysis, racial differences in Reasoning (B) scores become insignificant. Presumably, the longer one is in school, the more familiar and comfortable one becomes with certain forms of problem solving. (Too often, attempts to make intelligence tests "culture fair" do not consider the extent to which the testing situation itself is not culture fair.) Low scores from poor or uneducated clients should be interpreted in context.

Another source of variance is the client's ability to concentrate. Correct solutions to the Reasoning (B) items require not only intellect but also the ability to pursue a line of thought without becoming distracted. Situational anxiety or stress-induced preoccupation are examples of distractions based on circumstances. Personality traits that could interfere with concentration might include excessive anxiety or apprehension, poor self-discipline, or lack of focus. Thus, scores on Reasoning (B) may be negatively affected when the Anxiety (AX) global factor or Impracticality (M) is above average or when the Self-Control (SC) global factor is below average.

Low scores on Reasoning (B) must be compared to how clients would fare if they guessed at random. With 15 items and 3 choices, the client who guesses should get 5 items right on the average, which translates to a sten score of 3. The client who can figure out 1 item and guesses at the rest should receive a sten score of 4. Thus, low scores on Reasoning (B) may have less to do with intellectual ability than with other factors. The cognitive processes required by the items may be susceptible to the adverse effects of substance abuse, brain damage, emotional distress, or psychosis. Therefore, when a client's clinical presentation or education suggests above-average intellectual functioning but his or her Reasoning (B) score is below average, the clinician should consider impairment as an explanation. Comprehensive assessment of intellectual functioning may be indicated.

When the clinical presentation does not suggest above-average intellectual functioning, a low score on Factor B can be interpreted only as an absence of marked intellectual capacity. It may suggest a lack of motivation in taking the test or the possibility of fatigue (especially in regard to administration of the 16PF Fifth Edition on which all Factor B items appear at the end). On previous editions of the 16PF, air traffic controllers rated the Factor B items as the most objectionable on the test (Karson & O'Dell, 1974). Whether the topic is broached by the client immediately after taking the test or whether the clinician inquires after scoring the test, a conversation about the client's approach to these items can be enlightening.

The Reasoning (B) items represent the only facet of the 16PF on which the client is confronted with the possibility of failure. Such a possibility can stimulate an investment in doing well since most people are emotionally and even narcissistically invested in their intellectual abilities. Apathy toward the items often signals problems concerning investment of the self in work and in other spheres as well. Overinvestment also can indicate problems, including a variable sense of self-esteem and fear of failure. Treatment implications of a low score on Reasoning (B) often involve the need to show, rather than merely tell, the client how to do something and the need to avoid relying too heavily on the client's ability to assimilate verbal information such as interpretations, reconstructions, and abstract ideas.

High scores on this scale indicate superior reasoning ability and verbal facility. One cannot necessarily infer an absence of the kinds of things that can interfere with intellectual functioning, since even a high score may be lower than what a person's unimpaired ability would produce. A high score does indicate that in spite of whatever problems the individual may have, intellectual functioning is above average. Reasoning ability can make up for deficiencies in other areas. Cognitive strengths may be associated with the ability to defer impulses (". . . the native hue of resolution is sicklied o'er with the pale cast of thought . . . ." *Hamlet*), to anticipate contingencies, and to solve life's problems.

Factor C: Emotional Stability (Ego Strength)

Descriptors: Reactive, Emotionally Changeable (- pole) *versus* Emotionally Stable, Adaptive, Mature (+ pole)

Cattell called Factor C "Ego Strength," a name we much prefer to Emotional Stability. Originally a psychoanalytic term, ego has come to mean the executive functions of the personality, including reality testing and integration of various aspects of the self. Some of its Freudian meaning was lost when translators changed his *I* and *it* into the Latin *ego* and *id* (presumably to make them sound scientific). Ego Strength means that the parts of the self that most people identify with—those referred to when saying "I"—are not buffeted about, distracted, or overwhelmed by the things that people do not identify with, the things that just happen to them. These things include external forces and demands as well as a variety of internal events, including nightmares, competing agendas, and feelings that are difficult to admit. People low on ego strength are constantly coping not only with life's challenges but also with challenges from within. They are likely to find that their goals are not being pursued and met, that life is unsatisfying, and that their sense of self-esteem and well-being is suffering. The concept of low ego strength, by any name, implies disadvantageous functioning in an inefficient organism. Anxiety is a major indicator of this inefficiency.

Low scores on Ego Strength (C) are associated with a wide variety of psychopathologies, symptoms, and adjustment problems (Cattell et al., 1970, pp. 83-84). This is true partly because people with less ego strength are more susceptible to psychological problems and also because the items question self-adjustment issues. The fact that the items are fairly obvious allows the clinician to interpret low scores with some confidence, unless the client is suspected of having a possible motivation to look bad. Thus, low scores on Ego Strength (C) typically signify a desire to look bad, an attempt to communicate a need for help, or genuine adjustment problems. A desire to look bad may be inferable from the circumstances of the testing or from the score on Impression Management (IM). An IM score above the 20th or 30th percentile suggests that a low score on Ego Strength (C) is valid, since any effort to look bad would typically lead to a low IM score. Distinguishing a "cry for help" from low ego strength is difficult to do from the 16PF alone. Generally, if a psychosocial history does not reveal significant adjustment problems, then a low score on Ego Strength (C) should at least be considered as primarily reflecting a communication to the therapist (see chapter 2 regarding communicative versus measurement aspects of test scores).

Because of the obviousness of the scale's items, above-average scores on Ego Strength (C) indicate self-representations of ego strength more reliably than ego strength per se. Of course, many people will represent themselves as well-adjusted because they are, but others will do so for other reasons. The score on IM should invariably be considered in interpreting a high score on Ego Strength (C). If the score on IM is not very high, then a score on Ego Strength (C) is likely to represent genuine ego strength since the probability of faking good is reduced. However, IM not only is a simple measure of faking good but also is related to self-esteem and concern about what others think; therefore, people with ego strength can be expected to represent themselves positively. Indeed, Ego Strength (C) and IM correlate +.50 (Russell & Karol, 1994, p. 23). A high score on IM does not necessarily invalidate a high score on Ego Strength (C), and raises the possibility that both were elevated by desirable characteristics.

When a score on Ego Strength (C) is very high, above 7, it warrants skepticism. The highest possible sten score on this 10-item scale is 9, and achieving it requires responding to every item in the positive direction. A sten score of 8 is achieved by answering a single item with the "?" alternative and the rest in the positive direction. Thus, scores above 7, and especially above 8, indicate such insistent declarations of positive adjustment and ego strength that the clinician should question the need for such insistence, whether the client is protesting too much.

An interesting comparison can be made between Ego Strength (C) and another 9-point scale that simply asks clients to rate themselves from 1 (mentally unhealthy) to 9 (mentally healthy) (Katz, 1973). In one study (Karson, 1980), almost half of the clients rated themselves at 9. An analysis of these clients' 16PF profiles suggested that three kinds of people gave themselves the highest ranking, and these groups may be relevant to very high scores on Ego Strength (C). One group consists of those who are not open to acknowledging anxieties or psychological conflicts, either because they are trying to make a good impression or because they are too defensive. A second group includes people who are well-adjusted but not particularly mentally healthy in the developmental sense of identity integration, flexibility, and maturity. These people rank themselves high on mental health because they are symptom-free and adapted to their cultural and social niche. Their lack of symptomatology would not be a good predictor of their ability to meet novel challenges. Only the third group can be considered mentally healthy in the developmental sense of psychological growth (cf. Horney, 1950, or Maslow, 1968). Thus, very high scores on Ego Strength (C) may reflect the "illusion of mental health" (Shedler, Mayman & Manis, 1993) more than the genuine article.

The score on Ego Strength (C) is one of the cornerstones of our approach to interpreting a 16PF profile. Almost every other feature of the test varies in meaning according to Ego Strength (C), just as virtually any behavior can vary in meaning according to the ego strength of an individual. For example, ego strength signals the difference between magnanimous, sociable individuals and those who depend on the approval of others to insulate them from feelings of worthlessness (either of which would be reflected in high scores on Warmth [A]). As another example, among extremely socially bold (H+) individuals, ego strength accounts for the difference between those who are socially confident and those who compulsively seek the attention of others to compensate for feelings of insignificance. Both these examples involve extreme scores that do not in and of themselves suggest psychological problems. When Ego Strength (C) is used to shed light on such problem scores, its use is somewhat different. Thus, a combination of Ego Strength (C+) and very high Vigilance (L+) does not mean that the suspiciousness is expressed in a healthy form but that the externalization defenses are protecting the ego. In conjunction with problems in other areas, high scores on Ego Strength (C) suggest that a client's defensive maneuvers are successful, at least partly and temporarily.

The implications of Ego Strength (C) for psychotherapy depend on a client's score and psychosocial history. Low scores in an otherwise benign context may signal a willingness to make oneself available for the therapeutic process, especially for supportive or brief treatment. Low scores interpreted as problems in ego strength may indicate some difficulty in becoming objective enough to talk productively about problems and in developing a working alliance with the therapist. People with adequate ego strength often do well in psychotherapy, probably because they can apply that strength to problem areas or because their problems tend to be situational and transient. Very high scores on Ego Strength (C) may indicate a reluctance to acknowledge problems, which could be an impediment to treatment. In our experience, this reluctance is particularly associated with male clients.

Factor E: Dominance (Assertiveness)

Descriptors: Deferential, Cooperative, Avoids Conflict (- pole) *versus* Dominant, Forceful, Assertive (+ pole)

Since the 16PF Fifth Edition version of Factor E has more to do with assertiveness than with dominance, the former name for the new scale is our preference. The difference between the two names concerns the extent to which a person's motive is self-expression versus the control of other people. An assertive person wants to be heard, whereas a dominant person wants to be obeyed, to impose his or her will on others.[5]

High scorers like to let others know what they think, and are likely to cherish dominion over their personal space, their work, and their plans. They do not hesitate to express themselves or to stand up for their rights or point of view. In groups, they can be expected to play a larger role than average, taking up more air time and setting the agenda. They are noticed by others, and their willingness to speak up implies that either they expect others to be interested in their opinions or they do not care what others think. Their self-expressiveness makes them appear confident and competent. It is often their competence that makes them think that others will be interested in, or even deferent to, their opinions.

Although significant differences exist between dominance and assertiveness, their opposites have a lot in common. Low scorers are humble, submissive, and diffident. They are willing to "suffer the slings and arrows of outrageous fortune" rather than "take arms against a sea of troubles." Their lack of assertiveness causes them to envision others as uninterested in their needs or as antagonistic to having their needs met.

Facilitating group process at the expense of individual needs (i.e., not making waves) is how women frequently are socialized in many families and cultures. In other words, submissive women are more likely to find social support for their stance than are submissive men. Perhaps because of this issue, Factor E is one of the three 16PF Fifth Edition scales with different norms for men and women. These norms differ only on the low end of the scale, not on the high end. Thus, assertiveness is assertiveness, whether it occurs in a man or a woman; however, a woman's submissiveness is more likely to be a function of her position than of her personality, as compared to a man's submissiveness.

Assertiveness is a form of aggression, albeit a more sublimated form than dominance. High scorers are likely to be comfortable with their own aggression and with other people's as well. Low scorers are likely to be uncomfortable with aggression and reticent in confronting it since they anticipate that others' anger will be destructive. Moreover, they are so unfamiliar with their own anger that when they do become angry, they are awkward and unskilled in displaying it. Low scorers may be more explosive than high scorers, partly because they tend to bottle things up and partly because they lack practice in integrating anger with other factors. Very low scorers basically present themselves as sheep, that is, as less aggressive than any human can be. This suggests that their anger is disowned and unacknowledged, so that when it occurs, they are unprepared to express or deal with it.

Assertiveness (E) is especially interesting when considered in the context of couple's therapy. Although it is only the fourth most prominent factor in people's descriptions of each other's personalities (after A, B, and C), it is particularly relevant to dyads. Spouses find many reinforcers in the behaviors of each other, and naturally want to control the source of those reinforcers to assure their availability. This leads to a "jockeying for position" in many marriages. Many concepts of family therapy concern these efforts at mutual control. For example, "coalitions" can be viewed as attempts by the currently weaker spouse to garner support from a third party and to use the new relationship as a power base. "Structural ambiguities" may result when the spouse who seems to be losing the struggle attempts to change the rules of the contest.

Of course, the winning spouse does not always have the higher score on Assertiveness (E). Instead, the couple's scores are likely to indicate what they consider to be their equilibrium and how they struggle for control. High scorers are likely to make obvious power moves, ranging from asserting to arguing to intimidating. Low scorers are likely to create diversions, invent obstacles, and fight passively. An assertive (E+) wife pleaded, cajoled, and bullied her husband into agreeing to attend her company picnic, but when the big day came, he forgot about it and went fishing before she woke. When very high scorers are married to each other, there can be emotional fireworks, and attention must be paid to keeping the marriage contained within reliable boundaries.

Factor F: Liveliness

Descriptors: Serious, Restrained, Careful (- pole) *versus* Lively, Animated, Spontaneous (+ pole)

Because the 16PF factors correlate closely with one another, they become harder to distinguish individually as their placement in the list progresses. Liveliness (F) is a primary factor, but it also plays a part in other traits; several other factors correlate significantly with Liveliness (F) because one pole may require more energy than the other. For example, being sociable (A+) and bold (H+) takes more effort than being reserved (A-) and shy (H-). If the concept of liveliness is abstracted from all its manifestations, however, the essence of Liveliness (F) emerges.

Cattell et al. (1970) hypothesized that Liveliness (F) relates to an individual's history of punishment, assuming that a rewarding environment breeds optimism and enthusiasm about looking over the next horizon. Thus, people who were excessively punished for their behavior as children would be more cautious in their approach to the world around them.

Our view of the relationship between an individual's reinforcement history and Liveliness (F) is more complicated than Cattell's. On the low end, we tend to expect a history of extinction more than one of punishment. Low scorers are not so much fearful of negative consequences as they are pessimistic about effort producing reward. Some low scorers might claim that they are just being realistic. Indeed, Liveliness (F) is the factor on which age has the largest effect (Conn & Rieke, 1994, p. 45); younger people tend to be livelier than older people. This is partly because physical and mental energy levels decrease through young adulthood and perhaps partly because older people have seen more things go wrong and therefore are likely to settle for less.

On the high end, reliable reinforcement will produce only so much vitality and excitement. A history of punishment also will produce high energy levels since response tendencies are unleashed in the absence of the punisher. Thus, adolescents who get into trouble when away from home are more likely to be from families that punish than from families that encourage. High scores on this factor often signal not only liveliness but also immaturity and impulsivity. Ego Strength (C+), Compulsivity (Q3+), and the Self-Control (SC) global factor have to be considered to determine the difference.

Scores of 3 or 4 on Liveliness (F) can indicate a mature acceptance of responsibility or a pessimistic resignation. Discerning the difference is hard, just as distinguishing wisdom from inaction can be difficult. Again, Ego Strength (C+), Compulsivity (Q3+), and the Self-Control (SC) global factor can help somewhat. Using these indicators of emotional and behavioral control to color the interpretation of F+ makes more sense than using them on F-scores because the bridles of Ego Strength (C+), Compulsivity (Q3+), and the Self-Control (SC) global factor are what lively, happy-go-lucky people need. When Liveliness (F) is low, Ego Strength (C), Compulsivity (Q3), and Self-Control (SC) may be average or high simply because they are not challenged by strong impulses. Another possibility is that these traits may be too strong for the individual's own good. Instead of ego strength, the C+ score may signal difficulty in allowing feelings and impulses to emerge. The high score on Compulsivity (Q3) may indicate perfectionistic standards in the face of which the F- individual has thrown in the towel, rather than habit strengths that bolster the self in the midst of an emotional setback.

In our experience, very low scores on Liveliness (F) usually mean trouble. Equating these low scores with depression is impossible in part because depression is too complex a construct. Depression can involve hopelessness, sad feelings, and negative self-appraisal, but it also can involve agitation and a host of other lively methods to avoid sinking into despair. Another reason for the lack of a simple relationship between Liveliness (F) and depression is the difficulty of interpreting the score out of the context of other personality resources. Still, a very low score on Liveliness (F) raises questions about why the person is so uninterested in life, so somber and serious.[6]

To achieve a sten score of 1, the client cannot endorse even a single item in the lively direction. The extreme nature of such a score—beyond what most people could endure over time—often indicates a situational reaction to a setback, as if the client is admitting that he or she hates life and liveliness. Very low scores may be communications about feeling depressed more than actual indicators of depression. The reasons for such a communication vary according to the circumstances of the testing (Rahe, Karson, Howard, Rubin, & Poland, 1990). Sometimes, the client is alerting the clinician that help is needed. Or a low score may reflect the client's downward spiral of self-appraisal, which cognitive therapy often helps by demonstrating that the depression is not as deep as the client believes.

Factor G: Rule-Consciousness

Descriptors: Expedient, Nonconforming (- pole) *versus* Rule-Conscious, Dutiful (+ pole)

Rule-Consciousness (G) relates to "the degree to which people have been conditioned to conform to the ideals of their group, and how well they understand the rules of the social game" (Karson & O'Dell, 1976). High scorers are not only conscious of rules but also respectful of them. Rules may be valued for many reasons. They may summarize environmental contingencies, sparing each person in the group from having to discover adaptation strategies individually. In this form, rules transmit the knowledge and wisdom of a culture across generations, and it is hard to think of a reason not to value them. Rules also may be valued as instruments of authority in controlling the governed. In this form, people and cultures may vary widely in their appreciation of rules, ranging from Taoist distrust to Confucian reverence.

Like many 16PF factors, Rule-Consciousness (G) is most usefully conceptualized, at least from a clinical standpoint, as a discontinuous variable. Instead of a continuous dimension from nonconformity to conformity, the factor is a smooth linear variable only in its central range, with extreme scores being interpreted as not only quantitatively but also qualitatively different. Very low scores on G indicate that the client does not appreciate, or claims not to appreciate, any of the uses of rules in society. This may reflect a rebellious stance, typically associated with adolescent differentiation from the parents. It also may stem from an antisocial adjustment by which rules are viewed as mere obstacles to impulse gratification. Very low scores may signal Horney's (1950) resigned type, who escapes depression through the appeal of freedom. This type claims immunity to the demands of society because deference to those demands would make him or her feel trapped and suffocated.

Very high scorers who respond to the scale items honestly not only recognize the value of rules but also rely on them over their own experience. They tend to be moralistic; that is, whether they are approving or disapproving, they constantly hold up the behavior of themselves and others to an inflexible standard. They avoid negative self-appraisal by identifying with the appraiser. Very high scores are more difficult to validate than very low scores. A client who claims to value rules may be putting on an act. On the other hand, a client who claims not to value the rules of social conduct probably does not value them; consider that the client is willing to break societal expectations in his or her responses to the relevant test items. The Impression Management (IM) scale is of some help in determining the validity of a high score on Rule-Consciousness (G). Many people who genuinely revere rules will score high on IM because they do care dearly what others think about them.

Low scorers in the central range may be more inclined to cut their own path, rely on their own experience, and self-justify their behavior than relatively high scorers in the same range. The low scorers may not be as conscientious or as concerned with outward appearances as other people might prefer. They often require good rationales for behaving according to the expectations of others since they are not inclined to do so as a matter of course. This "why should I" attitude can be a strength when the individuals are hardy or when their social environment is flexible, but it can cause distress otherwise.

Factor H: Social Boldness

Descriptors: Shy, Threat-Sensitive, Timid (- pole) *versus* Socially Bold, Venturesome, Thick-Skinned (+ pole)

Factor H measures sensation-seeking versus being inhibited. Cattell et al. (1970) hypothesized that threat-sensitive, thin-skinned people develop behavior supplements for the management of threats by retreating in shyness rather than being exposed to risks. In contrast, thick-skinned people, whose agendas are not easily disrupted by threat-arousal, blithely venture forth into the social world. Like other social factors with problematic low scores (e.g., Warmth [A], Assertiveness [E], and Liveliness [F]), shyness (H-) can stem not only from preference but also from a punitive learning history. Experiences of social failure highlight the existence of threats, making shy people even more shy. Thus, the clinician must consider whether extreme low scores on Social Boldness (H) reflect a pathological withdrawal from social interchange. This desire not to be noticed can be difficult to distinguish from the emotional reserve of low Warmth (A-) and from the submissiveness of low Assertiveness (E-). In general, the A- individual withdraws by avoiding contact with people; the E- individual, by avoiding influencing people; and the H- individual, by avoiding being noticed by people. Since the factors are intercorrelated, the issue of avoidance tends to be more significant than its exact form.

Social boldness can be conceptualized as the willingness and interest required for the crossing of interpersonal boundaries. The archetypal situation for Factor H is the initiation of social contact with strangers. It is a powerful factor in sales effectiveness, and it also relates strongly to overt sexual interests (both of which involve crossing boundaries). Trial and error versus reflective problem solving can be equally effective strategies in many contexts, but socially, the bold individual who shrugs off failures will have more social successes than the cautious person who evaluates a situation before taking a risk. These successes will result in a number of rewarding contacts with others and a good fit in the contacts retained. In other words, socially bold people (and especially those who are also warm and assertive) are more likely to end up with friends and colleagues who really know them and like them than are socially restrained people. Social boldness pays off, especially if a person recovers easily from the occasional rebuff.

Part of what enables socially bold people to withstand failure is narcissism, or self-love. Narcissism can be primitive, meaning that it can derive from a denial of the feelings about and implications of social failures. Some socially bold clients pathologically process social failures not as reflecting badly on themselves but as reflecting badly on the people who rebuffed them. High scores on Social Boldness (H) also can signal a narcissistic preference for the early stages of a relationship, when the other person still interacts mainly with the social facade rather than with the whole self. However, most narcissism is more mature than this since it is based on a history of being loved by others and therefore leads to a robust sense of self-esteem and being a valued person. In fact, many socially bold individuals have internalized a sense of being loved to the point where being rejected by strangers simply loses its sting. Thus, high scores on Social Boldness (H) can signify narcissism but certainly do not suggest problems in and of themselves. At the other end of the scale, low scores always raise questions about whether the person feels that he or she possesses the reliable love of others, a requirement for venturing out into the social world.

High scores on the social factors are easier to distinguish than low scores. Warm (A+) people want to be around others, often in a caretaking, or at least, a friendly mode. Assertive (E+) people want to express themselves and influence others. Socially bold (H+) people want to be noticed and like to initiate interpersonal contact. These poles also are intercorrelated since all involve social contact.

Factor I: Sensitivity

Descriptors: Utilitarian, Objective, Unsentimental (- pole) *versus* Sensitive, Aesthetic, Sentimental (+ pole)

This factor might have been called "femininity," if not for the problems associated with that label, which also have plagued scale 5 (Mf) on the MMPI (with which Factor I invariably correlates moderately to highly) (Karson & O'Dell, 1987). Politically, the label of femininity sounds prescriptive of current values rather than descriptive of traditional values. Clinically, some people balk at being described as similar to the opposite sex. Practically, the words *feminine* and *masculine* change meaning from time to time and, especially, from culture to culture. Still, Factor I is the 16PF scale that maximally distinguishes the sexes. A man has to answer every item in the tough direction to receive a sten score of 1 (using the sex-specific norms); a woman can answer 3 of the 11 items in the tender direction and still receive a sten score of 1. The essence of the Sensitivity (I) scale lies in an item comparing an interest in football with an interest in poetry. Obviously, many women prefer football and many men prefer poetry, but these people are probably more androgynous than most. Androgyny, like any flexible approach to the world, can be a strength or a weakness, depending on overall adjustment. In relatively healthy individuals, flexibility implies the likelihood of responding advantageously to a given circumstance. In more fragile people, a reliable strategy for approaching problems and relating to others may be more advantageous than the potential morass that excessive options can produce. Thus, men who score very low on Sensitivity (I) and women who score very high not only may be strongly identified with a sex role in a particular culture but also may be sheltering some ego fragility behind a solid sex-role stereotype. Men who score high and women who score low may be inviting trouble by not maintaining a consistent social persona, or they may be exploring various ways of being in the world to achieve maximum satisfaction. The interpretation must be tempered by the recognition that variations exist from one subculture to another in what constitutes a refined and cultured person. A low score on Sensitivity (I) for a man who has spent his entire life in a New England college town may have a different meaning from the same score for a man who has spent his life on a west Texas ranch.

Cattell (1957) lists the following adjectives as descriptive of I-: "emotionally mature, independent-minded, hard, lacking artistic feeling, unaffected by 'fancies,' practical, logical, self-sufficient, responsible, free from hypochondria." Those associated with I+ are "demanding, impatient, dependent, immature, kindly, gentle, aesthetically fastidious, introspective, imaginative, gregarious, attention-seeking, frivolous, and hypochondriacal." The factor is close to what William James described as tender-minded versus tough-minded.

In therapy, I+ individuals tend to accept the idea of talking to someone about problems as a natural thing to do. They are conversant with feelings and do not need a lot of prodding to see the relevance of emotions to behavioral issues. On the other hand, they can be unusually sensitive in their reactions to criticism, and they may need confrontational interventions to be couched in a very accepting and supportive tone. They may interpret the therapist's professionalism as a distancing maneuver rather than as a way to keep the relationship safe. I- individuals are not likely to call a therapist to ask for help. Typically, they are either dragged in by family members or referred by work supervisors. They are likely to view the whole process as nonsense or as a threat to their competence and self-esteem. On the positive side, I- individuals usually respond well to a practical rationale for simple intervention strategies. They appreciate good logic, and once they decide to try a new approach, they do not mull it over or talk it to death like many of their I+ counterparts.

Factor L: Vigilance

Descriptors: Trusting, Unsuspecting, Accepting (- pole) *versus* Vigilant, Suspicious, Skeptical, Wary (+ pole)

In our experience, very high Vigilance (L) scores are one of the strongest indicators of psychopathology on the 16PF. A sten of 10 is achieved only if the client endorses the suspicious pole of every single item; a sten of 9 is not far behind. Suspiciousness, of course, is not always paranoid. To qualify as paranoid, the forces about which suspicions are harbored must be projections of some aspect of the self. Typically, paranoids are trying to explain frustrations and disappointments—their own anxious insecurity—by inferring a systematic accumulation of power by others against themselves. The basis for this fantasy is ubiquitous: everyone grows up in a situation in which others have extreme power and not all parents manage the power differential well. Thus, although suspiciousness and paranoia are not identical, extreme or pervasive suspiciousness is likely to reflect not the nature of society but the nature of the suspicious individual. Very high scores on Vigilance (L) also may signal a lack of awareness in regard to how the suspicions sound to most people or a lack of caring since the negative tone of the items is easy to spot. This reinforces the impression of a paranoid element to very high scores.

Naiveté is another common form of paranoia. Indeed, the MMPI-2 subscales for 6-Pa include persecution, poignancy, and naiveté. Naiveté plays a role in paranoia because in its pathological form, it depends on the denial and projective avoidance or expulsion of hostility. To be extremely trusting, people have to be exceedingly unaware of and unprepared for hostility. This level of denial may extend to their own hostilities as well. Very low scores on Vigilance (L), however, may not indicate pathological naiveté so much as an effort to make a good impression or a nonpathological belief in the goodness of others. Still, very low scores should at least be considered as possible paranoid markers, especially if a psychosocial history contradicts the professed level of trust (e.g., arrests, outbursts of rage, achievement in a competitive field). After all, some insist that Othello's tragic flaw was not jealousy but a blind trust that left him ill-prepared for his suspicions.[7]

In the middle range, Vigilance (L) is related to anger. The score provides an indication of how quickly an individual becomes angry, the amount of pent-up hostility carried around, and the extent to which others keep their distance. Vigilance (L) is also related to an interest in details as opposed to the big picture. Low scorers can miss the trees for the forest, and vice versa is true for high scorers. "Trifles light as air are to the jealous confirmations strong as proofs of holy writ" *(Othello)*.

The power differential in the therapy dyad may be difficult for high scorers to handle. They may require so much "democratizing" of the relationship that the therapist loses the leverage needed to bring about change. High-scoring men may balk at the discrepancy between their image of sex-role adequacy and the client role, much as I- men might. All high scorers may be inclined to sexualize the relationship with a therapist of the opposite sex (or the sex they are attracted to), as one mode of a general tendency to focus on the power in the relationship itself rather than on the reason for treatment. They are likely to become preoccupied with sexual fantasies about the therapist, to construe the encounter as a romance, and to focus on what the therapist thinks of them sexually. Treatment of low scorers often involves gentle probing of motives, their own and others', to develop comfort with and preparation for normal ranges of human aggression.

Factor M: Abstractedness (Impracticality)

Descriptors: Grounded, Practical, Solution-Oriented (- pole) *versus* Abstracted, Imaginative, Idea-Oriented (+ pole)

This factor is very different from its Form A counterpart, and clinicians who draw inferences about scores based on their experience with Form A are likely to be disappointed in the results. The Form A version of Factor M measured the location of the individual's focus of attention, ranging from a self-absorbed focus on the self to an external focus on the immediate environment. In its place, the 16PF Fifth Edition provides a measure of impracticality. High scorers acknowledge being impractical people, while low scorers claim to be practical. Since little about being impractical recommends it as a coping strategy or psychological adaptation, high scores may be indicative of psychopathology. Like some other obvious scales on the 16PF (e.g., low Ego Strength [C-], Expedience [G-] and Vigilance [L+]), the combination of obviousness and undesirability in high scores on Factor M suggests either an effort to "fake bad" or genuine adjustment problems compounded by a failure to recognize the undesirability of the trait. A parallel may exist between the inability to edit out the trait in the person's self-representation on the test and a difficulty in recognizing and addressing problematic behaviors in life.

In an industrial context, high scores on Impracticality (M), like low scores on Rule-Consciousness (G), are especially problematic, as all job applicants should know to represent themselves as practical. In a clinical context, high scorers may be trying to tell the clinician that they are dissociative, histrionic, hypomanic, or obsessional. Whatever the reasons for the impracticality, high scores bear further exploration. One inference that may transfer between Form A and the Fifth Edition involves the client's ability to attend to repetitive routines, like some factory work, all air traffic control, and other jobs that require sustained attention. While the situation is ambiguous on the low end of this scale, high scorers may be expected to have some difficulty with this kind of behavior. Corollary situations in other life spheres include many kinds of housework, monitoring children, and driving.

Interpretations of low scores on Impracticality (M) are complicated by the social desirability of many of the items. Low scores may be achieved by very down-to-earth people or by people who recognize that the opposite side of this coin is represented negatively in the items. In fact, the tendency to answer the items in the desirable direction constricts the distribution of stens so that one cannot achieve a sten of 1 on the factor and one must answer every item in the practical direction to achieve a sten of 2. Because test-taking attitude is so relevant to Impracticality (M), why it loads on the Self-Control (SC) global factor is unclear. Is it because practical people really are more controlled, or is it because the client, in achieving a low score, has exhibited self-control while taking the test?

Factor N: Privateness

Descriptors: Forthright, Genuine, Artless (- pole) *versus* Private, Discreet, Non-Disclosing (+ pole)

Casual encounters with N- individuals while at the park or in line for a movie are memorable experiences. They readily share the details of their lives with strangers: their latest romance, their boss's unprofessional conduct, their net worth, and their latest medical problems. Conversely, a clinician may spend months or even years with N+ clients before learning about their family secrets or their financial status. Obviously, these behavioral examples are complex, and being private (N+) is correlated with other factors to reflect that complexity. Private people also are likely to be reserved (A-), shy (H-), suspicious (L+), and self-sufficient (Q2+) (Conn & Rieke, 1994, p. 94), traits that can restrain self-disclosing.

Beyond the behavioral description of self-disclosing, very low scores may signal inexperience, hypomania, or narcissism. Low scorers have not learned an optimal degree of discretion for getting along in our culture, either because they have not been sufficiently exposed to the conditioning effects of groups (inexperience) or because they are inured to those effects by dint of their disdain for others (narcissism) or their own enthusiasm (hypomania).

A score in the middle range of this trait usually is not relevant to the clinician. An exception exists in couple's treatment, where some types of communication problems can relate to the partners' differences on Privateness (N). Partners with such differences may need to learn to appreciate, or at least tolerate, each other's preferences concerning self-disclosure to avoid interpreting the other's behavior as if it had the same meaning coming from oneself. Low scorers often think high-scoring partners are unhappy with them, since low scorers would only stop communicating to distance themselves from others (until they cannot stand it any longer and have to say what they think). Low scorers also may consider their high-scoring partners' ability to avoid immediately discussing every problem as a sign of not caring. Meanwhile, high scorers may perceive their low-scoring partners as intrusive and relentless in their pursuit of information sharing, prompting the high scorers to vigorously defend their privacy. The end result can be a vicious circle.

Factor O: Apprehension

Descriptors: Self-Assured, Unworried, Complacent (- pole) *versus* Apprehensive, Self-Doubting, Worried (+ pole)

In regard to Factor O, Karson & O'Dell (1976, p. 64) noted:

> Although scale O is considered by Cattell (1957) to be the least adequately defined of all the factors derived through the English language analysis, nonetheless our experience has shown this to be one of the most important scales on the 16PF from a clinical standpoint. A glance at the items shows again and again the anxious worrying and guilt that is associated with many clinical syndromes, including depression and obsessive thinking. Feelings of vague dread, guilt without reason, extreme reaction to criticism, fear of punishment, and poor self-esteem, all associaed with O+, are the bread and butter of many therapists.
>
> The adjectives listed by Cattell (1957) as descriptive of this factor show roughly the same thing. O- adjectives include "self-confident, self-sufficient, accepting, tough, and spirited." O+ adjectives are "worrying, lonely, suspicious, sensitive, and discouraged."
>
> Clinical experience with this scale has shown that scores other than the average signal disturbance all too frequently. That is, either O- or O+ scores bear investigation.

Thinking of psychological dynamics as patterns of internal dialogues between different aspects of the self may be helpful. In that context, Factor O relates to the quality of the relationship between internalized authority and the "I." Low scores often mean that the conscience is not active or not being listened to, leading to fewer pangs of guilt. Of course, some people may be so well-behaved that their consciences never upbraid them, but this is rare. High scores on Apprehension (O) suggest that the conscience is hostile to the individual and is accusatory without reason. Of course, some people recently may have behaved badly, leading to excessive remorse.

Antagonism between conscience and identified self is a character-
istic of depression and, indeed, O + often indicates depressive
trends, especially if Liveliness (F) is low. Depression can be
seen as succumbing to a hostile internalized authority. When
Liveliness (F) is high, the antagonistic self-appraisal often leads to
counter-depressive acting out, thwarting the internalized authority
with which the individual cannot make peace.

Like the obsessive thinking it resembles, Apprehension (O+) is
resistant to therapeutic efforts to change it. Telling someone not
to worry does not help. Further, arranging extinguishing consequences for the behavior is difficult because it is so divorced from
external effects; instead of the behavior being demonstrated as
useless, practically any outcome seems to justify worrying. Often,
the therapist may find focusing on another problem to be more
productive, assuming that change in another arena will give the
client less to worry about. Arranging for satisfying compromises
around impulse expression leads to a reduction in worrying more
reliably than a frontal attack on the worrying itself. The therapist
must remain alert to the possibility that worrying will come to
dominate the therapy sessions and drive out more productive
topics, analogous to the way worrying can play a defensive role in
the client's thinking by distracting energy and attention from more
disconcerting problems.

The "Q" Factors

The last four of the 16 primary factors were discernible only on
questionnaire data, not from behavioral ratings. This most likely
occurred because three of them—Openness to Change (Q1),
Compulsivity (Q3), and Tension (Q4)—are about largely internal
experiences and because the fourth, Self-Reliance (Q2), is too
much like Warmth (A) to distinguish in vivo. They appear on
questionnaire data because only the individual is able to provide
information about certain private states. Cattell, the pure
researcher, felt that these traits should not receive the same status
as those derived from direct observations, and therefore distinguished them with the "Q" (for questionnaire) label. Our clinical
experience has been that there is no need to downplay the contributions of these factors to the personality makeup of clients.

Factor Q1: Openness to Change

Descriptors: Traditional, Attached To Familiar (- pole) *versus*
Open To Change, Experimenting (+ pole)

This scale has changed dramatically from its previous Form A version, and clinicians should avoid using defunct inferences. Cattell et al. (1970) speculated that it was only a sign of the times that the old version of Q1 conflated openness-to-change with political radicalism and hostility to authority (the latter being the central interpretation of the Form A version). With the passage of the era of the Great Society and Vietnam, change and antiestablishment attitudes are no longer equivalent, and the Fifth Edition items relate only to the former.

Except for very low scores, which can signal trouble, this trait can be interpreted as a straightforward measure of an individual's attitude toward change. The higher the score, the more oriented the person is toward trying something new; the lower the score, the more directed the person is toward making do or savoring what is available. This trait needs to be considered within the context of the person's current satisfaction with life. Some low scorers are too quick to settle for too little; some high scorers cannot appreciate how good they have it. High scorers sometimes need help evaluating conditions since they tend to overrate their prospects and underrate their status. Therapists can help these people develop alternative methods of experiencing and enjoying innovation that enable them to satisfy their quest for change without relinquishing what they already have.

The relationship among openness to change, current circumstances, and depression is exemplified by the old story about two boys trapped in a room filled with horse manure. One boy, identified as the pessimist, sits glumly, while the other boy, identified as the optimist, happily shovels manure while declaring, "There must be a pony in here somewhere." On reflection, which is the pessimist and which is the optimist is unclear. The second boy has accepted the condition of a room filled with horse manure and is making the best of a bad situation; he is optimistic about finding a pony but pessimistic about change. Meanwhile, the glum boy is holding out for better conditions. This conundrum arises frequently in clinical work, where often the healthiest family members show depressive symptoms in response to family dysfunction.

Very low scores on Openness to Change (Q1) may indicate problems with flexibility and adjustment. Low scorers may resist change for reasons that go beyond a pessimistic tendency to "make do" or a mature capacity to savor what is available. Instead, they may have a history of being unable to adapt to novel circumstances gracefully. A severely constricted identity definition (or array of possible roles to play), analogous to a personality disorder, may underlie an excessive resistance to change. People expressing such resistance may sense that they will not fit in under new conditions and so cling to the familiar. Beyond this hypothesis of identity constriction, very low scores also may reflect a history of aversive experiences that have made avoiding pain more important than pursuing satisfaction. Any such history is more likely to be associated with psychopathology than a history of gratifications.

A difference on Openness to Change (Q1) is often of significance in couple's therapy. The low scorer's anxiety about change may lead to a perception of the high scorer as immature or irresponsible, while the high scorer may view the low scorer as a stick-in-the-mud. The high scorer does not realize that his or her innovations bulldoze the low scorer's savoring; the low scorer does not realize that his or her attachment to the familiar deadens the high scorer's anticipation. Typically, each partner has to learn to empathize with the other's mode of enjoyment and to find ways of indulging his or her personal preferences in ways that do not impose on the other's.

Factor Q2: Self-Reliance

Descriptors: Group-Oriented, Affiliative (- pole) *versus* Self-Reliant, Solitary, Individualistic (+ pole)

This factor's name is a bit misleading since its positive connotations make the low end of the scale seem unduly negative. The factor could be renamed "Team Player Versus Loner" since it addresses an individual's tendency and preference to do things alone as opposed to doing them with others. In fact, Self-Reliance (Q2) can be considered as an activity-oriented version of Warmth

(A). The higher the score, the more solitary the person. In our experience, many people answer the items on this scale according to their work lives and respond to the items on Warmth (A) according to their personal lives.

Interpretation of scores must consider the client's general level of competence. Many people who do not perform a given task well prefer to work in groups so that their inadequacy is not obvious. Conversely, many people who excel at a given task become frustrated when collaborating with others who are less adept. For these reasons, Self-Reliance (Q2) scores can be affected by the client's competency level or degree of self-confidence. However, there is not a simple relationship between competence and Self-Reliance (Q2), especially since the items cull clients' preferences rather than their requirements. Many people who prefer to work on teams can work alone if necessary and vice versa.

Very high scores on Self-Reliance (Q2) can signify trouble in regard to interacting comfortably with others. Extremely solitary people, like extremely reserved (A-) people, are likely to be actively avoiding others rather than just expressing a proclivity for being alone. They may be especially prone to seeing others as slow or as inefficient. When circumstances force them into collaborative relationships, they often do not respond well. A therapist for a very high scorer can spend months trying to establish a cooperative atmosphere or a working alliance without achieving any emotionally authentic interchanges. In this situation, the therapist has to avoid exacerbating the client's distancing by engaging in excessive pursuit. The client may interpret the therapist's efforts to create a rapport as a sign of the therapist's incompetence. Identifying this interpretation to the client can be a powerful move and a sign of strength for the therapist.

Self-Reliance (Q2) contributes to the Extraversion (EX) global factor, and its meaning needs to be understood in the context of the other extraversion factors. Relatively high scores suggest self-sufficiency and task-mastery, but if other extraversion indicators are also low, even a moderately elevated score on Self-Reliance (Q2) is likely to represent merely an aversion to collegiality. Conversely, high scores on Self-Reliance (Q2) more clearly suggest desirable self-reliance when other scales indicate that the person is globally extraverted.

Very low scores should raise questions, but not necessarily conclusions, about being overly dependent on other people. The clinician must consider whether low-scoring clients prefer to do things with others because they cannot stand on their own. Several dependency paradigms could account for such a fear, including fear of failure or fear of success, either of which makes people want to hide in a crowd.

Factor Q3: Perfectionism (Compulsivity)

Descriptors: Tolerates Disorder, Unexacting, Flexible (- pole) *versus* Perfectionistic, Organized, Self-Disciplined (+ pole)

According to Cattell et al. (1970), Compulsivity (Q3) represents:
> . . .the level of development of the conscious, behavior-integrating self-sentiment, i.e., the extent to which the person has crystallized for himself a clear, consistent, admired pattern of socially approved behavior, to which he makes definite efforts to conform. The degree of attainment of this self-ideal pattern is, of course, not measurable very validly by questionnaire. What we are here measuring is the amount of concern and regard for these standards.

Like Horney's (1950) concept of the idealized self, perfectionistic standards can inspire or tyrannize, depending on the emotional connotation associated with not living up to them. An absence of perfectionistic standards can mean freedom from tyranny or just stagnant complacency, depending on other factors.

Horney named three major types of perfectibility under which fall the neurotic functioning of most relatively healthy people. She called these the appeal of mastery (associated with moving against other people), the appeal of love (moving toward), and the appeal of freedom (moving away). From Horney's perspective, to arrive at the concept described by Cattell would require items aimed at each type of perfection. Instead, the Fifth Edition's Perfectionism (Q3) items define what might be called a British version of perfection: orderliness and good habits. Thus, we believe the Fifth Edition name is overly broad and prefer Compulsivity, which retains the perfectionistic notion that too much can be almost as bad as too little.

Compulsivity (Q3) is related to identity integration versus identity diffusion, but not in a simple way. People with diffuse identities are apt to score low or very high. They are likely to score low as an indicator of their familiarity with and tolerance of disorganization and chaos. External chaos does not rub them the wrong way. On the other hand, some people with identity diffusion may compensate for inner vagueness with superficial intactness (Deutsch's [1942] "as if" personality). These people need extra insulation from external chaos, and are likely to score extremely high on Compulsivity (Q3). In general, then, low scores raise questions about why the person has not developed useful habit strengths. A likely answer is that identity coherence is lacking, and with it, a desirable degree of predictability. Low scorers have to reinvent the wheel on each new occasion.

A very high score raises questions about why the person needs so many habits. Do the habits replace personhood? In addition, extreme compulsivity always raises concerns about anger: the thicker the bars on the cage, the wilder the beast within is assumed to be.

Compulsivity (Q3) is usually a good indicator of the ability to bind anxiety. At the same time, too high a score on Compulsivity (Q3)—especially when coupled with Vigilance (L+) and Rule-Consciousness (G+)—can indicate undue rigidity. Productive and creative people often score high on Compulsivity (Q3), although very high sten scores (8 or above) are unusual in these people. Our experience indicates that when anxiety is too tightly bound, creativity and flexibility may suffer. Certainly, the Q3+ person is not going to tolerate much ambiguity or disorder in life, and disorder is often essential at some stage of the creative process (Karson & O'Dell, 1976).

A Q3- person would experience difficulty in performing success-fully within a large corporate or government hierarchy that rewards responsibility and compulsivity. Should low scores on Compulsivity (Q3-) be coupled with the other anxiety indicators, a safe assumption is that the person is in distress. This person likely is unable to organize his or her impulse life to enable the constructive use of energy rather than its dissipation (Karson & O'Dell, 1976).

Generally, Compulsivity (Q3) is most useful as an indicator of ability to control emotions, particularly anger and anxiety. Indeed, Compulsivity (Q3) proved to be one of the best discriminators on the 16PF when a sample of mothers of disturbed children was compared with a matched sample of mothers of better adjusted children (Karson, 1960). A useful analogy may exist between the management of emotions and the management of children, and Compulsivity (Q3) would represent, when not in excess, one of the better ways of achieving both.

Factor Q4: Tension

Descriptors: Relaxed, Placid, Patient (- pole) *versus* Tense, High Energy, Impatient, Driven (+ pole)

The personality trait referred to by this factor is associated with free-floating anxiety and generalized frustrations. Tension, thus construed, can lead to anxious behaviors (e.g., insomnia, rumination, fidgeting, and nervous habits) as well as to behaviors associated with a depleted frustration tolerance (e.g., impatience and irritability). Cattell et al. (1970) note that distinguishing Tension (Q4) from problems in Ego Strength (C-) and Apprehension (O+) is not always easy, and indeed, the three scales are intercorrelated. In general, we think of Apprehension (O+) as guilt-proneness and negative self-appraisal and of Tension (Q4+) as relating more to the tensions and anxieties associated with insecurity, a paucity of suitable avenues for self-expression, and an excess of environmental demands compared to internal resources. Tension (Q4) and Ego Strength (C) are interrelated because the greater the ego strength, the greater the internal resources available to cope with demands and the greater the likelihood that the individual has developed avenues for self-expression.

As a scale, considered separately from the trait, Tension (Q4) is fairly transparent. This makes it highly susceptible to the communicative and self-representational aspects of the testing enterprise (see chapter 2). Tension (Q4) is easily faked, can be used as a communication to the referral source, and is affected by a person's conscious self-concept. These sources of variance cannot be disentangled from the effects of the underlying source trait in interpreting a given score. In our experience, when clients emphasize how they want to appear over how they tend to be, extreme scores are obtained. Thus, very low and very high scores are more profitably interpreted as communications than are middling scores.

The communication behind low scores is that the client is emphatically not in distress. In certain settings, like custody evaluation, such scores are expected and perhaps even desirable, since they may represent an understanding of what is expected and a willingness to play along. In treatment settings, the intensity of the refusal to acknowledge anxiety symptoms must be questioned. Sometimes, very low scores mean that the client is psychologically unprepared for tension and may not handle it well when it arises. At the least, a client who scores very low is unlikely to be easily engaged in treatment. The low score can represent a poor prognosis, not only because the client may not accept its relevance but also because anxiety can be a good motivator. Often, it is advisable to explore whether someone else is behind the referral for therapy and to consider inclusion of that person in the treatment.

Our experience indicates that except when a client may have a blatant reason for faking bad, a very high score represents both the presence of the source trait and a desire that the tester or referral source should know about it. In some jobs, this may be an adaptive stance of acknowledging stress levels. Indeed, some businesses go so far as to actively construe impatience as a virtue since it implies that the individual has important things to do. Tension also is seen as a sign of importance and commitment in many jobs. People who value stress typically immerse themselves in it and often need help justifying relaxation and recreation.

Clinically, high scores on Tension (Q4) usually mean experiential trouble and are often the prime focus for treatment. Tension (Q4) scores typically correlate highly with Scale 7-Pt (Psychasthenia) from the MMPI (Karson & O'Dell, 1987). Like Scale 7-Pt, Tension (Q4) is a measure of subjective distress, but sometimes being in distress is a better sign than not. This is true when life has taken a bad turn or when other symptoms are prominent. Subjective distress can be a good sign because it can indicate that some part of the individual is discomfited by disasters and symptoms and also because it can indicate some motivation to change things for the better.

CHAPTER 5
RESPONSE SET OR VALIDITY SCALES

Psychological testing depends on standardizing or controlling stimuli so that differences among subjects can be revealed. True standardization requires not only that the external stimulus be the same for everyone but also that the internal motivational set be as uniform as possible across subjects. This is why the 16PF (or any test) should not be administered when a client is having a panic attack or undergoing trying circumstances and why at least minimal rapport should be established with a client prior to test administration. Use of norms depends on a similarity between the motivational set of the reference group and the test-taker or at least an effort to account for the differences.

Personality assessment by questionnaire may be especially vulnerable to a distorting influence on scores induced by variations in response sets across clients. In contrast, when motivational influences affect responses in so-called projective tests, the clinician typically records, questions, and interprets expressions of those influences. With personality inventories, the clinician, except on rare occasions, has only the scale scores as a source of information. Therefore, the testing circumstances must be considered when the scores are interpreted. Independent efforts to assess motivational set and the client's orientation to the test also are provided on the 16PF.

The validity or response set scales of the 16PF Fifth Edition assess the test-taker's attitude toward the test and attempt to check for influences other than the desired self-descriptions according to item content. The Impression Management (IM) scale focuses on the level of social desirability in the responces to items, raising a flag about possible client efforts to look better or worse than could be realistically expected. The Acquiescence (ACQ) scale tries to measure the client's tendency to agree with item statements regardless of their content. The purpose of the Infrequency (INF) scale, which consists of item responses least frequently chosen by the norm sample, is to detect random responding, poor comprehension of the items, and general deviance.

IMPRESSION MANAGEMENT (IM) SCALE

Impression Management (IM) consists of 12 items relevant to socially desirable behavior in our culture. The scale includes absurdly self-congratulatory items (e.g., indicating that one has never hurt another's feelings), reasonably defensive items (e.g., denying moods of self-pity), and mainstream socially acceptable behaviors (e.g., not making foolish remarks just to disorient others).

The main purpose of the IM scale is to assess the client's tendency to respond in socially desirable ways, so that other scale scores can be interpreted in the context of whether the client responded forthrightly to items or in a manner suggesting concern about what others might think. IM also has an interpretive significance in its own right. A client's desire to manage the impression being made on the 16PF can relate not only to what the relevant professionals may think, but also to the client's general investment in others' opinions. The latter, in turn, relates to interpersonal engagement, self-esteem, and good judgment. Thus, under most test-taking circumstances (except those where the client might have an obvious reason to look bad), IM can be construed as a measure of test-taking attitude as well as of social comprehension and self-esteem.

Very high scores on IM depend on the client endorsing the entire mix of items. Consequently, such scores indicate more than just good judgment and self-esteem; they suggest that the client may have made a concerted effort to look good. Altering other scores to reflect this tendency is not recommended, making the 16PF Fifth Edition different in this respect from the 16PF Fourth Edition and the MMPI; however, otherwise positive indicators on the test do need to be interpreted cautiously when IM is very high. The factors most affected by any motivational distortion would be those most highly correlated with IM: IM correlates higher than .30 with Ego Strength (C) and Rule-Consciousness (G), and lower than -.30 with Vigilance (L), Impracticality (M), Apprehension (O), and Tension (Q4) (Conn & Rieke, 1994, p. 64).

When IM is very high and when negative or socially neutral extreme scores are achieved on other scales, useful inferences can be derived. These stem from the observation that even though the individual probably attempted to look good, certain scores were obtained. Therefore, negative indicators would suggest some questions about the individual's judgment or about his or her ability to recognize certain behaviors as undesirable. For example, an extremely high IM score coupled with a low score on Compulsivity (Q3-) may indicate that the client's disorderliness and disorganization are so ego-syntonic that he or she cannot recognize them and edit them from the self-presentation.

Extreme scores on more neutral scales often indicate that a client has a peculiar definition of what is construed as socially desirable. One client scored extremely high on IM and in the socially desirable direction on every other 16PF scale. She also scored very low on Self-Reliance (Q2). Consequently, the clinical interpretation centered on her evident belief that dependence on others was a socially desirable trait, which provided a key insight into her self-concept and her attachment to an unrewarding marriage.

Very low scores can signal an effort to look bad, problems with self-esteem and social involvement, or both. Low scorers may be indifferent to or downright scornful of the clinician's opinions, the referral source, and in all probability, the social network. They may be willing to sacrifice their social standing to influence the test results, to convey their negative self-appraisal, or to express their disenfranchisement from socially desirable behaviors. Whatever the actual reason, their willingness to forgo a positive social persona suggests psychological and adjustment problems that need to be fully explored in the clinical dialogue.

Acquiescence (ACQ) Scale

This scale consists of nearly all the 16PF items having true-false (a-b) response choices. On the 16PF, the true alternative always appears first and thus is designated as the a choice on the answer sheet.

The hypothesis giving this scale its name—that acquiescent people tend to agree that item stems are true about them irrespective of item content—is supported by the data.[1] High scorers are more submissive (E-), shy (H-), and trusting (L-) than low scorers, and high scorers also are less warm (A-), lively (F-), sensitive (I-), impractical (M-), open to change (Q1-), orderly (Q3-), and tense (Q4-) than low scorers. While these traits do not combine to form a perfect portrait of acquiescence, the key elements represented by the first three factors mentioned (E, H, L) are all in the expected direction.

When Acquiescence (ACQ) is very high or very low and the scores on its associated factors do not support the interpretation, the ACQ score likely represents random responding or poor comprehension; the scale will identify a subject who is inclined either to choose or to avoid choosing the *a* response alternative for whatever reason. Such a protocol could be of limited interpretive use. When a more modest ACQ score is supported by scores on its associated factors, it can be viewed as a supplementary indicator of excessive agreeableness.

INFREQUENCY (INF) SCALE

Infrequency indices on personality inventories, such as F on the MMPI, are designed to detect random responding, general deviance, and poor reading comprehension. Interpretation of infrequency on the 16PF Fifth Edition is complicated by the test structure. Except for the Factor B items, the middle response alternative (labeled *b*) is always a question mark *(?)*, a choice that represents the "uncertain or cannot decide" option and which the test-taker is instructed to select as infrequently as possible. The 32 items comprising the INF scale are keyed in the *b* response direction since no other response alternative to any item is chosen infrequently enough to qualify for this scale. As a result, the clinician needs to consider why a client chose the *b* alternative an excessive number of times apart from those reasons for which the Infrequency (INF) scale was designed. One possibility is that the client is oppositional, deliberately choosing to flout the test instructions and to act noncompliantly. Another is that the client is wishy-washy about answering the questions or determined not to be self-revealing. Finally, the client may have misunderstood the intent of the question mark as a response alternative, instead selecting it to indicate that he or she did not understand the meaning of an item. Typically, these hypotheses are supported by other 16PF scores. The oppositional client often is assertive (E+) or suspicious (L+); the ambivalent client, worried (O+) or disorganized (Q3-); the nondisclosing client, private (N+); and the uncomprehending client, verbally limited (B-).

CHAPTER 6
GLOBAL FACTORS

Technically, the global factors were derived by putting 16PF test results on the primary factors through a factor analysis. Whereas the 16 primary factors are an optimal number of traits accounting for variations in how personality is described by the English language, the global factors are 6 traits that optimally account for how people differ on the 16 factors. One of the 6 global factors is intelligence (Factor B), held over relatively unchanged from the basic 16 factors (and not discussed here). The other 5 global factors resemble the "Big Five" personality factors that some theorists consider the important dimensions of personality.

The global factors of the 16PF Fifth Edition are called Extraversion (EX), Anxiety (AX), Tough-Mindedness (TM), Independence (IN), and Self-Control (SC). These factors, like the 16 primaries, exist in a mathematical space defined by factor analysis. During the analysis, they were assigned labels to assist in their conceptualization. The intent was not to measure the important dimensions of extraversion per se, anxiety per se, and so forth. This is a subtle but important distinction for the practicing clinician. Knowing a client's overall score on the global Anxiety (AX) is useful for understanding how the client's scores on certain primaries (C, L, O, and Q4) have been affected by the global factor. The clinician's real interest lies not in the client's score on the Anxiety (AX) global factor but in the approximation of his or her overall mental health that can be derived from the 16PF.

There may not be (and in our opinion, there is not) a complete correspondence between the mathematically derived factor named "anxiety" and the clinically relevant concept of mental health by any name (including neuroticism, emotional adjustment, dynamic integration, or psychological development). In our opinion, a better approximation of overall mental health can be obtained by looking at not only global Anxiety (AX) but also the number of problematically deviant scores on certain factors and at scores that convey compensating strengths (especially Compulsivity [Q3], global Self-Control [SC], and global Extraversion [EX]).[1]

However, for practicing clinicians to use formulas concocted for relevant concepts like "overall mental health" or "dependability" would be highly questionable without supportive research. Someday, a series of studies may show that adding Compulsivity (Q3) to the global Anxiety formula or Ego Strength (C) and Apprehension (O) to the global Self-Control formula provides an improved real-life approximation of mental health and dependability, respectively. Until that research exists, the clinician is advised to rely on the global factors; however, in interpreting the global scores for individual clients, there is nothing wrong with considering other scores as well.

The main advantage of the global scores for the clinician is that they are based on many more items than are the primary factor scores, and consequently, are more reliable (Conn & Rieke, 1994, p. 81). The primary factors, except Reasoning (B) (15 items) and Openness to Change (Q1) (14 items), are based on 10 or 11 items each. By contrast, each of the global factors is based on from 40 items (Anxiety) to 51 items (Extraversion). Therefore, no single item has much effect on a global score, and the global scores are more robust than the primary sten scores. As a result, more confidence can be placed in global scores than in primary scale scores. Using global scores is especially important for any purposes that involve applying decision-making algorithms to groups of clients. For clinicians, global scores tend to be most useful as a summary of trends, especially scores on Extraversion (EX), Anxiety (AX), and Tough-Mindedness (TM). We do tend to use global scores for Self-Control (SC) and Independence (IN) fairly routinely in our interpretations of 16PF Fifth Edition profiles. For example, we have more confidence in the Self-Control score than in any of its components in estimating an individual's capacity to rely on habits and on impulse control when more integrative defenses are weakened. Independence, we find, is the best overall measure of aggressiveness on the 16PF. (These interpretations are examined more fully later in this chapter.)

The disadvantage of using the global scores is that they can disguise important elements in a personality. For example, a score of about 8 on Extraversion (EX) would be obtained from each of the following patterns:

	Client 1	Client 2	Client 3
Warmth (A)	2	10	8
Liveliness (F)	9	9	7
Social Boldness (H)	8	2	8
Privateness (N)	2	4	4
Self-Reliance (Q2)	2	4	5

In spite of sharing the same Extraversion (EX) score, the three clients have very different scores on the global's component factors and thus different portraits. Client 1 evinces little genuine warmth but appears to have an energetic and compulsive need to be near others. Client 2 seems to cling to others to avoid a sharp fear of rejection. Client 3 appears to be warm, outgoing, engaging, and socially effective. The point is that a person's score on a global factor does not convey as much information as do the scores on the global's component factors. As an analogy, consider how full scale IQ scores are most useful when there is little underlying scatter between subtest scores and little difference between verbal and performance scores. When the underlying scatter is great enough, too much information is lost by relying only on the aggregate score. And yet, reliabilities are highest for full-scale IQ scores, and they are often better predictors than subtest scores.

EXTRAVERSION (EX)

Descriptors: Introverted, Socially Inhibited *versus* Extraverted, Socially Participating

Jung first identified extraversion as a concept for understanding human personality. On the 16PF, Extraversion (EX) involves being warm (A+), lively (F+), socially bold (H+), forthright (N-), and group-oriented (Q2-). Cattell et al. (1970) speculated that all these factors are intercorrelated because they tend to affect one another. In other words, expressions of warmth are likely to garner social reinforcers (e.g., affection, approval, and attention), inclining the individual to be less shy (more H+), more enthusiastic (F+), and feel less need for privacy (less N+). Expressions of shyness (H-),

72

as a contrasting example, are likely to lead to being ignored by others, inclining the individual to be more reclusive (A-), private (N+), and self-reliant (Q2+).

Many of the interpretations of Warmth (A) apply to Extraversion, especially with extreme scores. A score below 3.5 on Extraversion (analogous to a score of 3 or less on a primary factor) should prompt concerns about possible pathological withdrawal. In interpreting a low Extraversion score, the clinician should inspect the extremity of the score, indicators of overall adjustment problems, and signs of problems with aggression. A more extreme score is more likely to reflect pathological withdrawal than a mildly deviant score. Indicators of overall adjustment problems suggest that a low Extraversion score, like any deviant score, is more frequently an expression of pathology than of preference. Finally, a very low Extraversion score is more likely to be troublesome if it is associated with problems with aggression (i.e., if the withdrawal seems to be a compromise tactic to manage extreme anger or extreme subduedness).

Extreme scores on the high end of Extraversion, like those on Warmth (A), suggest an identity organized around interpersonal relationships. In our culture, this kind of adjustment is not likely to signal psychopathology or adjustment problems, but the existence of a defensive purpose behind the extraversion should be considered. Horney (1950) divided neurotic behavior into three types: moving toward, moving against, and moving away from others. Those who manage feelings of unlovability by defining a perfectionistic ideal of social acceptance and trying to achieve it will score very high on Extraversion. On the other hand, those who are socially successful, fun-loving, and generous will score very high too.

ANXIETY (AX)

Descriptors: Low Anxiety, Unperturbed *versus* High Anxiety, Perturbable

Cattell et al. (1970) called this global factor "Anxiety versus Dynamic Integration," which gives a better sense of its approximation to emotional adjustment or overall mental health than the Fifth Edition label. In a large-scale study (N = 1915), Krug (1994)

reported a correlation of .50 between Anxiety and Depression, a second-order factor from IPAT's Clinical Analysis Questionnaire. This finding supports the interpretation of Anxiety along broader lines than one specific symptom complex.

With the exception of Reasoning (B), any 16PF Fifth Edition factor could be logically inverted so that low scores could be considered the high end of the trait. This is communicated by use of the terms "left" and "right" instead of "low" and "high." Anxiety is the only global factor for which this matters clinically. Our profession has more unitary names for the desirable end of this continuum (e.g., health, adjustment, integration, growth, development) than for the undesirable end, probably because our interest in people's problems has resulted in a more differentiated lexicon of problems than of resolutions. On the computerized 16PF Karson Clinical Report, we subtract the Anxiety score from 11 and call it by one of its desirable names. This fits better conceptually, since our use of the score tends to concern the "amount" of strength it represents, not the amount of difficulties.

Many similarities exist between the meanings of Ego Strength (C) and Anxiety; however, Anxiety scores are based not only on low Ego Strength (C-) but also on Vigilance (L+), Apprehension (O+), and Tension (Q4+). Because so many of the items from the latter three scales concern symptoms (as opposed to strengths), the Anxiety score can be improved easily (i.e., lowered) by a denial of problems. In our industrial work, we use Anxiety as an estimate of overall mental health (while also considering the number of problem scores and compensating strengths). We have yet to find a job where better-rated employees score higher on Anxiety than worse-rated employees; indeed, the opposite is almost always true. Anxiety's potential usefulness, like all the global scales, is enhanced by its having many more items than Ego Strength (C).

A high score on Anxiety either means that the person is overwhelmed or that he or she is acknowledging a lot of problems. The score on Ego Strength (C) and the number of problematically deviant scores (see p. 18) in the entire profile also need to be considered. For example, an elevation of Anxiety caused by high scores on Apprehension (O) and Tension (Q4) likely would indicate only transitional problems if Ego Strength (C) were average or high, if Vigilance (L) were not too high, and if no other adjustment problems are suggested by deviant scores. (The latter are called "areas to explore" on the 16PF Karson Clinical Report.) If no precipitants were discernible, the person still would be considered to be in turmoil and a chronic problem might be inferred, but his or her overall mental health would not necessarily be questioned. On the other hand, a high score on Anxiety based primarily on low Ego Strength (C-) and Vigilance (L+) would be of enormous concern; extreme scores in the indicated directions on the 16PF Fifth Edition are probably the gravest signs of long-term adjustment problems.

A low score on Anxiety also has to be investigated relative to its components. If such a score is based on a denial of problems (e.g., with Apprehension [O] and Tension [Q4] at a sten of 2), it does not provide much reassurance that the individual has reliable psychological resources. If a low Anxiety score is coupled with average or nearly average scores on the symptom-sensitive Apprehension (O) and Tension (Q4), then an elevation on Ego Strength (C) is less likely to be defensively based, and the Anxiety score is more likely to indicate actual psychological strength. In other words, given that higher scores on Apprehension (O) and Tension (Q4) imply a higher score on Ego Strength (C) if Anxiety remains constant, our interpretation of Anxiety is mediated by the Ego Strength (C) score. Extreme anxiety is likely to be situationally based, and situationally treatable, if Ego Strength (C) is average or high. Indeed, in a therapy assessment, some degree of Apprehension (O) and Tension (Q4) is expected and even desirable. This indicates that the individual is bothered by the situation compelling the therapy and is motivated by discomfort to engage in therapeutic tasks.

The Impression Management (IM) score also should be consulted in interpreting the Anxiety score. In fact, the entire 16PF profile can be viewed as an effort at impression management or identity definition; however, the kind of impression management that affects the IM scale—that related to social desirability—most strongly affects answers to the kinds of items on the scales that make up Anxiety. IM's correlations with Emotional Stability (C), Vigilance (L), Apprehension (O), and Tension (Q4) are its highest of all the 16 primaries. These scales' items concern strengths and weaknesses that are among the most sensitive in our society (possibly excepting intelligence, which is difficult to fake on an inventory). Therefore, if IM is average or low, the clinician can put confidence in a low score on Anxiety. However, the converse is not true; a high IM score does not invalidate a low score on Anxiety (although it does raise questions). This is because the kinds of healthy, well-adjusted people who should score low on Anxiety also tend to possess the kind of concern for the opinions of others and the kind of positive self-regard that increase IM scores. Even though a relatively high IM score does not invalidate a low Anxiety score, an excessive elevation on IM should raise suspicions since this score would have to include some or all of the IM items that are ludicrously self-congratulatory.

Tough-Mindedness (TM)

Descriptors: Receptive, Open-Minded, Intuitive *versus* Tough-Minded, Resolute, Unempathic

Even more than scores on other 16PF scales, a score on this global is of clinical interest only when it is extreme. The scale consists of weights on being reserved (A-), not sensitive (I-), practical (M-), and resistant to change (Q1-). Conversely, low scorers are some combination of warm (A+), sensitive (I+), impractical (M+), and open to change (Q1+). Most of the clinically relevant issues associated with Tough-Mindedness are investigated most profitably by examining the scale's components. For example, an important clinical issue involves the distinction between emotionality that stems from ego weaknesses and emotionality that stems from comfort and conversance with feelings. Tough-Mindedness, other mental health factors being equal, clearly involves the latter. It does so as a result of the contributions of Sensitivity (I) and Warmth (A), and therefore only those two scales need to be examined in this context.

In general, Tough-Mindedness has more industrial than clinical applications, but the former can offer some insight into the scale's nature. Air traffic controllers score, and should score, very high on Tough-Mindedness. Indeed, its original name was "Cortertia," which Cattell derived from "cortical alertness," and air traffic controllers would be poorly suited to their jobs if they were distracted by emotions or depended on intuition. Airline pilots also score high on Tough-Mindedness.

Clinically, an extremely high or low score does not imply pathology, but may suggest adjustment problems. Many of the
interpretations for Sensitivity (I) are applicable. For example,
low-scoring men and high-scoring women on Tough-Mindedness
may have trouble integrating this trait with their sex-role identifi-
cations, especially if they are from families or subcultures that
narrowly define masculinity as "tough-minded" and femininity as
"receptive." Any high-scoring individual may have trouble fitting
into some communities, from liberal arts colleges to social work
programs, and low scorers may find themselves at odds with
prevailing norms such as military values. High scorers will
require a no-nonsense approach in psychotherapy, if they come at
all. Low scorers may thrive on the culture in therapies that
emphasize feelings, and may take to it so well that they, and their
therapists, forget that there is an overarching purpose to the
sessions.

INDEPENDENCE (IN)

Descriptors: Accommodating, Agreeable, Selfless *versus*
Independent, Persuasive, Willful

Independence is comprised of weights on Assertiveness (E+),
Social Boldness (H+), Vigilance (L+), and Openness to Change
(Q1+). Previous editions of the 16PF call the low end of this
factor "Subdued," which we prefer because it connotes some of
the problems associated with low scores. Low scores are based on
some combination of being submissive (E-), shy (H-), trusting (L-),
and resistant to change (Q1-). Many of the interpretations of
Assertiveness (E) apply to Independence. While interpreting 16PF
Fifth Edition results, we rely more on Independence for signaling
problems with anger than on any other scale, although extremely
low scores on Assertiveness (E) and Social Boldness (H) or
extremely high scores on Vigilance (L) are interpreted as indicating problems with anger in and of themselves.

A good deal of anger can be sustained without becoming problematic by well-functioning people having Extraversion scores that are
not too low and Anxiety scores that are not too high. For these
people, high scores on Independence are probably best equated
with one of anger's socially desirable names, such as competitive-
ness (still a positive term in industry and sports), independence, or

will. If other scores or other sources of information raise questions about an individual's interpersonal connections or overall adjustment, a high score on Independence can signal a pervasive aggressive stance that constantly challenges interpersonal alliances or ego integration or both.

A very low score on Independence frequently indicates problems with anger for the same reasons described in our discussion of Assertiveness (E) (see p. 40). In short, a mismatch exists between the person's self-image and the fact that he or she is a member of a very aggressive species. This mismatch is likely to cause, and probably has been caused by, interpersonal (or psychosomatic) problems.

SELF-CONTROL (SC)

Descriptors: Unrestrained, Follows Urges *versus* Self-Controlled, Inhibits Urges

This scale is based on low Liveliness (F-), Rule-Consciousness (G+), Practicality (M-), and Compulsivity (Q3+). People who respect rules, consider the practical consequences of their actions, and desire to maintain order are likely to exhibit self-control. The livelier they are, the more they have to control and the more likely they will lapse. These considerations justify naming this mathematically derived factor Self-Control.[2] However, a thorough prediction of self-control also should include ego strength, overall adjustment, and susceptibility to guilt. One definition of *ego strength* is the "ability to defer needs," which is obviously related to self-control. Overall adjustment is important as an indicator of how much a person stands to lose if he or she acts impulsively. Feelings of guilt also can be important potential inhibitors. Indeed, Apprehension (O) probably does not appear on this global factor only because extreme scores in either direction weaken self-control. A high score indicates the undermining of a person's sense of well-being and the likelihood of impulsive acts, while a very low score suggests deficient constraints of the sort that are normally based on avoiding feeling guilty.

We have noted that an alarming number of criminals, addicts, and child abusers score high on Self-Control, and this leads us to speculate that the factor should be renamed "control" or "persistence."

The "control" label would correspond with the AA theory of alcoholism, which identifies the desire for control as a main contributor to addiction. Our experience is that much child abuse also stems from an unrealistic desire for control, one to which children are unable to conform. Extremely high scores on Self-Control, like those on Rule-Consciousness (G) and Compulsivity (Q3) individually, can signal control problems, since inflexible standards lead to a bottling up and eventual explosion of impulses. Even moderately high scores may be found in impulsive people. This makes us think that the scale may be better considered an index of interest in control; that is, a typical picture of the individual rather than the clinically interesting issue of the individual at his or her worst.

If Self-Control is really persistence, then its association with some drug abusers and criminals might not be that meaningful (although this label avoids the obvious contradictions of Self-Control with these people). However, the concept of persistence (or relentlessness) matches well with our clinical experience of people high on this global factor mustering the necessary resources to behave according to a plan, even if the plan is not always desirable. The factor appears to be related to the capacity to discharge the instrumental acts of goal-directed behavior, from getting up in the morning to clearing the in-basket to filing taxes (to getting a fix).

Another interesting interpretation views Self-Control as a measure of good habits. Mythically wise spiritual leaders are often represented in stories as being very low on self-control; they are so developed and integrated that they do not need custom to keep themselves on course. The rest of us can fall back on good habits when things become confusing or our resources are strained. Even a moderately low score can indicate a constant need to keep coming up with unique solutions to life's demands, which may exert an unneeded challenge to the person's adjustment.

CHAPTER 7
FACTOR INTERACTIONS

Score combinations of particular interest to the clinician are discussed in this chapter.* Some relate to factors whose effects compound each other; some, to factors that form a clinically useful dimension in conjunction with one another; and some, to factor scores that appear to contradict each other. The latter can seem to create interpretive difficulties, such as when a client scores high on both Privateness (N) and Warmth (A) or on any two scales normally correlated inversely. A global factor seeming to conflict with one of its components (e.g., a high Extraversion [EX+] score and a low Warmth [A-] score) is usually the result of a contradiction among the various primaries rather than between the specific primary and the global. Instead of considering such score combinations as bothersome idiosyncrasies, the clinician should view them as opportunities to discover the special aspects of the client's personality profile.

THE INFLUENCE OF THE FACTOR B SCORE

Two sets of interesting score combinations can be treated en masse. These involve Reasoning (B) and the amalgam of Ego Strength (C), global Anxiety (AX), and the number of problem scores approximating overall adjustment (see p. 18). Analogous to listing mental deficiencies and personality disorders on a separate axis for diagnoses, these factors create a context in which virtually every other factor score changes meaning.

Reasoning (B) can be expected to influence resourcefulness, impulse control, and competence. High scorers on Factor B

---

*The interpretive hypotheses in this chapter are based more on clinical experience and less on research than those presented in previous chapters.

generally are assertive (E+) and Self-Reliant (Q2+). When they are submissive or group-oriented, their use of their intellectual resources should be examined. If high scorers on Reasoning (B+), Assertiveness (E+), and Self-Reliance (Q2+) are also self-disclosing (N-), they can be expected to play a prominent role in most groups. If their Reasoning (B) is not high enough, they may annoy other group members by taking up air time disproportionate to what they are able to contribute. Another example concerns an individual who scores low on Impracticality (M-) and is therefore grounded in immediate reality. While examining this profile, the clinician must consider whether the groundedness makes the person practical (B+) or plodding (B-). The Private (N+) client is discreet, which can translate into worldly and shrewd (B+) or merely uncommunicative (B-).

THE IMPACT OF ESTIMATES OF OVERALL ADJUSTMENT

Estimates of overall adjustment affect virtually every factor interpretation. Overall adjustment relates to a person's abilities to hold conflicts in abeyance, to defer needs, and to behave under the influence of long-term consequences. We base estimates of overall adjustment on Ego Strength (C), global Anxiety (AX), Compulsivity (Q3) or global Self-Control (SC), and the number of problem scores (see p. 18). Ego strength means the difference between integrating impulses with life's other agendas and gratifying them thoughtlessly. Overall adjustment also distinguishes ability from proclivity, neurosis from choice. For example, extremely reserved (A-) people with low Ego Strength (C-) usually are unable to interact effectively with others. Those who are extremely reserved (A-) but have adequate or high Ego Strength (C) are likely to interact adequately with others when forced by circumstances; their normally reserved behavior is most accurately conceptualized as a preference.

Interpretations of Specific Score Combinations

Warmth (A) and Assertiveness (E)

The degree of Warmth (A) often affects the expression of Assertiveness (E). When both Warmth (A) and Assertiveness (E) are high, the latter often is smoothly integrated with social awareness. High scorers on both factors are more likely to be persuasive rather than stubborn or domineering when taking a stand on an issue. The latter less socially facilitative modes of self-expression usually are employed by assertive (E+) individuals who score low on Warmth (A).

When Assertiveness (E) is low, the degree of resentment associated with blocked aggression is likely to be great if Warmth (A) is also low. If Warmth (A) is high and Assertiveness (E) is low, the person may have found a satisfying stance from which to deny aggression. The lack of self-expression may be compensated by approval from others for being easy to get along with. Warmth (A+) and submissiveness (E-) still represent the culturally prescribed stance for many women, and women who do not fit the pattern may experience conflicts resulting from their challenging version of sex-role identification.

Warmth (A) and Social Boldness (H)

These two Extraversion factors usually agree with each other, and therefore, departures from this expectation require exploration and explanation. Social boldness (H+) without warmth (A-) is often associated with a tendency to prefer the initial stages of relationships over the long haul. Such scorers impress others but do not follow through with the level of attention and energy that relationships often require. A state of having many acquaintances but few friends can be produced by the reserved (A-) and socially bold (H+) combination.

An alliance of warmth (A+) and shyness (H-) is also unusual. The generosity of such scorers can combine with their unobtrusiveness to make them dependable friends, and frequently, they are organized around being caretakers of others. They may feel left out when their desire for companionship is frustrated by their inhibitions about pursuing it.

Warmth (A) and Sensitivity (I)

Both of these factors involve the expression of emotions. Warmth (A) usually relates to concern for other people's feelings, whereas Sensitivity (I), to an interest in expressing one's own feelings. The emotionality of Warmth (A) is more interpersonally based than the emotionality of Sensitivity (I), which also can reflect emotionality expressed in fantasies, beliefs, and values. People scoring low on sensitivity (I-) and high on warmth (A+) may express an interest in other people's feelings that is observant, thoughtful, or even akin to a parental role but does not involve their personal feelings. Often, the combination of I- and A+ is expressed as an interest in positive, and perhaps superficial, emotional exchanges among "hale fellows well-met."

When Sensitivity (I+) is associated with a low (A-) score on warmth, it tends to reflect the sensitivity for which it is named rather than the typically inferred expression of feelings. Individuals scoring in this manner are often thin-skinned. They have to avoid people or limit emotional exchanges with them to create a social buffer as a substitute for the nonexistent psychological one.

Warmth (A) and Vigilance (L)

Finding high scores on Vigilance (L) and Warmth (A) in the same profile is unusual since the suspiciousness, irritability, and hostility associated with L+ scores usually drive away other people. If Vigilance (L) is only slightly elevated, it is more representative of anger than of paranoia, and a good dose of warmth can offset some of the social effects associated with ready displays of anger. A high Warmth (A) score coupled with a moderately high Vigilance (L) score likely reflects an anger that does not fully objectify its targets. When Vigilance (L) is only moderately elevated, somewhat low scores on Warmth (A) need not raise concerns about anger; instead, the pairing seems like a natural balance. Since this person does not have much tolerance for others, his or her being reclusive and reserved in the presence of others makes sense. (In the latter example, if Reasoning [B] is also high, the client probably "does not suffer fools gladly.")

When Vigilance (L) is extremely high, very little can mitigate its seriousness. The combination of high warmth (A+) and excessive suspiciousness (L+) suggests a tendency to lure others into relationships that turn out to be artificial and fragile and, often, opportunities to vent hostility.

Warmth (A) and Privateness (N)

A low score on Privateness (N) generally is paired with an average or high score on Warmth (A). This makes sense for the childlike quality of self-disclosure can then be sustained by a warm social network. If Warmth (A) is also low and overall adjustment appears adequate, the person probably operates very differently alone versus when he or she is around others. This person is frank and indiscreet when opportunities arise, but may not seek out such opportunities. The presence of others may constellate intense sibling, dependency, or narcissistic issues, which may account for the difference between the person's social behavior and solitary behavior. The combination of extremely low warmth (A-) and privateness (N-) scores indicates confusion about how to relate to others and possibly some interchangeability of object relations, as exemplified by those desperate individuals who collar strangers on long plane rides.

Warmth (A) and Self-Reliance (Q2)

These scales are quite similar, with high scores on Warmth (A) associated with low scores on Self-Reliance (Q2). We have found that discrepancies between the scales often relate to a split between how people function socially (Warmth [A]) and how they function at work (Self-Reliance [Q2]). When it is not too high, the self-reliance aspect of Q2 also suggests that A+/Q2+ represents a desirable adjustment of social warmth with a capacity to accomplish a job independently. An average or high score on Warmth (A) and a high score on Self-Reliance (Q2) usually signify authentic self-reliance rather than difficulty in collaborating; the Warmth (A) score indicates there are some spheres in which the individual does interact positively with others.

When both scores are low, conflict usually exists. For example, A-/Q2- individuals may sense their dependency needs but not know how to satisfy them. Another hypothesis is that these people, who are naturally reserved and reclusive, are driven to join groups to accomplish projects because they feel personally incompetent (especially if Reasoning [B] and Assertiveness [E] are not high).

Assertiveness (E) and Liveliness (F)

Generally, people low on both Assertiveness (E) and Liveliness (F) are more likely to be passive-aggressive than those who are low only on Assertiveness (E). These people also can be sullen and immobilized in addition to harboring the resentment associated with low E- scores on assertiveness alone. When Assertiveness (E) is low and Liveliness (F) is high, hysterical trends may be observed. The same might be said more generally of low scores on Independence (IN) and high scores on Extraversion (EX). The combination of E- and F+ suggests that the individual is so cheerful because aggression is being denied or, conversely, that high activity levels are distracting the individual from his or her anger.

Assertiveness (E) and Social Boldness (H)

Like the combination of E- and F+, that of E- and H+ may represent an hysterical adjustment, with an interest in the opposite sex or an interest in making a splash (H+) replacing the excitability and cheerfulness of F+. The E+ and H- pairing is unusual, in that standing up for oneself (E+) is difficult without drawing attention to oneself. People with this score combination often assert themselves by being stubborn. Changing their minds is difficult because they tend to keep their emotional distance from the argument, and therefore, the opposite viewpoint has little impact on them. From their point of view, their assertiveness constantly involves them in tussles that their shyness would rather avoid, and significant inner conflict usually results.

Assertiveness (E) and Vigilance (L)

These two modes of expressing aggression are important to compare. In its broadest sense, assertiveness tends to be a form of anger expressed in the service of a goal independent of the relationship with the object of aggression, and therefore, it dissipates quickly when the inconvenience is removed. The irritability associated with mild elevations on Vigilance (L) and the hostility associated with extreme elevations are not so easily satisfied. When people who score high on Vigilance (L) get their way, they remain angry. For them, anger is not primarily in the service of a separate goal; instead, their anger serves an interest in being seen as people to be reckoned with, in achieving power over others, and in externalizing a sense of weakness. If Vigilance (L) is not high, then positive inferences about Assertiveness (E) as a healthy expression of aggression are likely to be true. Invariably, the clinician also would look for signs of overall adjustment.

Assertiveness (E) and Privateness (N)

Most people who are submissive (E-) and private (N+) are law-abiding citizens; however, this factor combination also was achieved by several corporate thieves whom we tested. Perhaps this trait pairing causes aggression to be expressed in a devious manner. The admonition to "watch the quiet ones" captures the idea that the resentment associated with E- eventually will be expressed in some indirect way when Privateness (N) is high. By the way, many of the thieves also scored low on Apprehension (O), which suggests deficient "superego introjects" or self-monitoring.

Liveliness (F) and Rule-Consciousness (G), Impracticality (M), and Compulsivity (Q3)

Distinguishing between impulsive immaturity and lively enthusiasm is important when Liveliness (F) is high. Estimates of overall adjustment represent the best way to do this, but reviews of Self-Control (SC) and its components also are helpful. Rule-Consciousness (G) helps bridle enthusiasm by making it conform to rules of conduct. Compulsivity (Q3) balances the lively (F+) tendency to act without due consideration. A low (M-) score on impracticality does not constitute a check on liveliness (F+), but a high score (M+) strongly indicates that the person's flights of fancy get out of hand occasionally.

Liveliness (F) and Social Boldness (H)

High scores on these two factors signify a sense of high energy levels, thrill-seeking, and intolerance for boredom; low scores on both indicate passivity and hopelessness. When scores on the two factors disagree, Liveliness (F) often provides a window into the inner life, while Social Boldness (H) may represent the social manifestations of activity versus boredom. The H+/F- person may be counterdepressive, trying to mask inner gloom with social excitement. The H-/F+ combination suggests immaturity and shyness, not as apparently contradictory as the H+/F- combination.

Liveliness (F) and Apprehension (O)

The F-/O+ combination signals a common form of depression characterized by low energy levels and self-recriminatory behavior. The opposite combination, F+/O-, indicates impulsivity, especially when either score is extreme. Although liveliness per se is a fine quality, it can cause psychological bumps and bruises; therefore, most people learn to monitor their behavior more carefully than do O- individuals.

Rule-Consciousness (G) and Impracticality (M)

How can a person be both rule-conscious and impractical? One answer is that the impracticality represents a problem, and the rule-consciousness an attempt at a solution. If so, the solution will be short-lived and marked by intermittent failures because it is directly opposed to the response tendency. Oblique solutions are more likely to produce lasting compromises than are head-on resolutions to avoid engaging in problematic behaviors. Another perspective on the conflict intrinsic to a G+/M+ combination considers the conventionality of Rule-Consciousness (G) as the preferred mode of the psyche's dominant forces and the Impracticality (M) as representing a kind of psychological guerilla warfare against the rigid system of behavior. Whether the combination is punctuated as beginning with the high score on Rule-Consciousness (G) or with that on Impracticality (M), therapy needs to focus on bringing the two tendencies into harmony via relaxing inflexible standards and committing to more thoughtfulness. Therapy for this kind of internal conflict resembles a kind of couple's therapy in that two sides need to learn how to coexist.

Rule-Consciousness (G) and Apprehension (O)

A combination frequently found on the 16PF Fifth Edition is a low score on Rule-Consciousness (G) and a high score on Apprehension (O). Such individuals are attempting to prove disregard for the standards of society while simultaneously admitting intense guilt that contradicts their apparent disregard. Although they understand how the game is played, they are trying to circumvent the rules and suffer guilt at their lack of conformity. Such a pattern is common in adolescents, who often rebel against their parents' standards but nevertheless feel guilt over the conflict. Therapists' consulting rooms are filled with such people. The challenge for therapists will be to hold up a mirror to these clients so they can see what they are doing in their relationships. They then may change the situation, breaking the vicious circle of nonconforming behavior followed by overwhelming guilt. Clinical experience suggests that Rule-Consciousness (G) is more easily modified than Apprehension (O); that is, the client may be helped to realize that the price paid for unconventional behavior is simply not worth the subsequent painful guilt feelings (Karson & O'Dell, 1976).

Rule-Consciousness (G) and Compulsivity (Q3)

These factors represent the two main strategies that most people use to supplement ego strength: conformity to external norms and expectations (G+) and internalizing them to bind anxiety (Q3+). As noted in chapter 4, either in excess can cause as much trouble as they normally relieve because of the rigidity associated with extreme elevations on each. If Compulsivity (Q3) alone is quite low, it implies a shallowness to behavior controls; the individual is likely to be merely imitating behavioral controls instead of having internalized them. If Rule-Consciousness (G) alone is low, the interpretation is more complicated. Signs of other strengths— including overall adjustment (adequate or high Ego Strength, low global Anxiety, few problem scores, and adequate global Self-Control) and Extraversion (implying social supports)—could mean that the low score on Rule-Consciousness (G) represents creativity, free-spiritedness, and nonconformity rather than problems with self-control.

Social Boldness (H) and Privateness (N)

Just as with all the other Extraversion factors, these scales make
the most sense when they point in the same extraverted (H+/N-)
or introverted (H-/N+) direction. When they do not, they usually
deserve comment. The H+/N+ combination often signals an
experienced or seasoned mode of interacting with others. For
example, good politicians are polished at initiating interpersonal
contact (H+) but consider carefully the impact of revealing personal data. In contrast, H-/N- individuals are shy and yet self-
disclosing. This can create a "dump and run" pattern, where they
share distressing information with others and then avoid them.
As a result, they may be surrounded by people whose knowledge
of their intimate lives intimidates them.

Sensitivity (I) and Vigilance (L)

A man's extremely low score on sensitivity (I-) suggests a stereotypi-
cal masculine style. The combination of an I- score and an elevated
Vigilance (L) score may indicate that the man is patrolling his environment for signs that his macho adjustment is not fully accepted
by others. The anger associated with high scores on Vigilance (L)
may be used to make doubters back off. In women, the I-/L+ combination also suggests an angry solution either to self-questioning or
to others' inquiries about femininity and sex-role adequacy. For
both sexes, a pairing of I+/L+ reflects a thin-skinned sensitivity to
real or imagined slights to the person's position of power, and this
may impel the person to lash out at others.

Impracticality (M) and Compulsivity (Q3)

Although this factor combination has more industrial than clinical
applications, it is still worth mentioning. People who are low on
impracticality (M-) and high on compulsivity (Q3) are usually good
at following a regimen and executing routines. Their minds rarely
wander, and if Liveliness (F) and Social Boldness (H) are not high,
they can repeat behaviors for a long time without losing interest.
Some clinical concerns may appear if a mismatch exists between
people's strengths or weaknesses in this area and the demands
made on them in the course of a day.

Apprehension (O) and Tension (Q4)

Although these two measures of discomfort or distress are fairly highly correlated on the 16PF Fifth Edition (r = .34, Conn & Rieke, 1994, p. 94), they certainly are not identical. Differentiating one scale from the other might be easier if other names were to be used for them, such as "worrying" (O+) and "impatience" (Q4+). Apprehension (O) tends to relate to pangs of conscience, self-reproach, and obsessing, while Tension (Q4) concerns how tightly wound a person is. A client receiving a low score on Apprehension (O) and a high score on Tension (Q4) can be described as anxious or impatient but not guilt-ridden or obsessive. A client receiving a high score on Apprehension (O) and a low score on Tension (Q4) may be described as worried but not impatient or tense.

Chapter 8
Case Studies

To illustrate use of the 16PF Fifth Edition as a clinical assessment device, this chapter presents a variety of 16PF profiles and their interpretations. Two examples concern the role of the 16PF as an integrated adjunct to brief treatment, which we believe will become a major clinical use for the test. Often, a particular profile is not as salient as the conversation that it stimulates and, indeed, one of the main advantages of the 16PF in the clinical setting is that it is easy to discuss with clients.

Profiles were selected for inclusion in this chapter because they are interesting or revealing. Background information has been slightly altered to provide client anonymity. With the exception of the first and last cases for which the 16PF was used as part of brief treatment, assessments involved the administration of other tests in addition to the 16PF. For most adult clinical problems, we typically administer the Bender, Rorschach, Early Memories, and either the Shipley (a brief intelligence test) or the WAIS-R. Additional tests are administered as needed.

Certain cases were not presented in this chapter because their profiles would be of interest only in conjunction with other sources of data. For these, the 16PF raised few or no concerns about serious psychopathology, although the psychosocial history or other testing did contain pathognomonic indicators. This combination usually indicates a capacity to function well in the more superficial and cognitive psychological space occasioned by answering inventory items as compared to poorer functioning in the more intimate, inner psychological space occasioned by so-called projective tests.

Whenever possible, we pursue follow-ups on our assessments, and when available, they are reported for the case studies included in this chapter. We believe that failing to discover what transpires after an assessment hinders a psychologist from continuing to learn how to tailor his or her interpretations to reality. This situation is analogous to trying to learn how to bowl without ever looking down the alley to see which pins were knocked down. Bringing one's assessment behavior under the influence of reality requires feedback.

CASE I: MR. A, AGE 21

REFERRAL

This self-referred college senior, majoring in communications, had never been on a date. His striking good looks stood in contrast to the presenting problem. He stated that his best friends were all women but they were just that—friends—and nothing more. Although he had been kissed by women while dancing or talking at numerous parties, he denied ever initiating the kissing.

During the first session, Mr. A explained he was seeking help because he was "terribly worried" that there was "something wrong" with him. He expressed concern that he might be gay, even though he denied ever having a sexual thought about a man and claimed to have an active fantasy life focused on women. He described an incident that had occurred on the day he had decided to seek therapy. A desirable woman appeared to be flirting with him after class, but he could not find the words to suggest a date and merely excused himself. The therapist, concerned that social skills were the problem, asked Mr. A what he should have said in retrospect. Mr. A replied, "Hey, I was about to get a cup of coffee. Do you want to come along?" Both Mr. A and the therapist agreed that knowing what to say was not the problem. The 16PF was administered at the conclusion of the first session.

MR. A's 16PF PROFILE

PRIMARY TRAITS

Factor		Sten
A	Warmth	7
B	Reasoning	8
C	Ego Strength	6
E	Assertiveness	4
F	Liveliness	5
G	Rule-Consciousness	8
H	Social Boldness	5
I	Sensitivity	8
L	Vigilance	4
M	Impracticality	6
N	Privateness	4
O	Apprehension	5
Q1	Openness to Change	7
Q2	Self-Reliance	5
Q3	Compulsivity	6
Q4	Tension	3

RESPONSE SET SCORES

Scale		Percentile
IM	Impression Management	57
ACQ	Acquiescence	47
INF	Infrequency	51

GLOBAL FACTORS

Scale		Sten
EX	Extraversion	6.3
AX	Anxiety	3.6
TM	Tough-Mindedness	3.1
IN	Independence	4.6
SC	Self-Control	6.6

PROFILE INTERPRETATION

The therapist showed the profile to one of us, who said, "Looks like a healthy guy, lots of friends, a bit of a sweetie-pie. He can get pretty moralistic about what a sweetie-pie he is, but other than that, lots of strengths."

These comments require some annotation. The estimate of overall adjustment (i.e., "looks like a healthy guy") is based on the average Ego Strength score (C = 6), above-average scores on the globals Extraversion (EX = 6.3) and Self-Control (SC = 6.6), the below-average score on global Anxiety (AX = 3.6), and the absence of problem scores. "Lots of friends" is implied by the Extraversion score and the absence of any suggestion of social problems from its components (e.g., no excessive shyness). The "sweetie-pie" designation refers to the ambivalence about aggression implied by the low Independence score (IN = 4.6) and the feminine qualities associated with Sensitivity (I = 8) and low Tough-Mindedness (TM = 3.1). Since the commenting psychologist grew up on the "mean streets," he does not consider being a sweetie-pie much of an advantage in life. The remark about getting "pretty moralistic" derives from the score on Rule-Consciousness (G = 8). In and of itself, this score suggests some moralistic tendencies, but in a profile with no other scores that are more deviant, it likely represents a fairly prominent aspect of Mr. A's self-presentation.

SUBSEQUENT SESSIONS

The therapist began the second session with the 16PF answer sheet and profile sheet in plain sight, determined to bring the test results into the conversation at some point but not wanting to supersede Mr. A's agenda. In fact, Mr. A began the session by asking, "So am I crazy?" The therapist replied, "Au contraire, but let's look at some of these scores together." After explaining the profile sheet (see Appendix C) and dispensing with the positive indicators, the therapist pointed out the low score on Tough-Mindedness (TM = 3.1) and the high score on Sensitivity (I = 8). Mr. A, understanding the concepts, discussed his comfort with women as opposed to most groups of men, adding that he never played or even watched sports and had no interest in "macho stuff." The therapist wondered to himself if Mr. A had come to define making love to women as "macho stuff." (The therapist used the Anglo-Saxon term in his own mind, and eventually, in conversation with Mr. A to emphasize that the client had come to consider sex as being rude and crude.)

Prior to the latter occurrence, the therapist discussed the high score on Rule-Consciousness (G = 8). In response to the thera-pist's analogy of doing what is "correct" versus what comes naturally, Mr. A made an association with political correctness. He acknowledged that when he was with a member of the opposite sex, a good deal of his energy and attention was devoted to remembering to call her a "woman" and not a "girl." To minimize the potential conflict between the therapeutic goals and the client's belief system, the therapist explained that he was not questioning the values underlying political correctness. The therapist did lament the difficulty encountered in trying to be politically correct while feeling lustful. This observation inspired a conversation that carried over into the third session; it was aimed at justifying male lust in the context of Mr. A's political beliefs. The dialogue culminated in the therapist's effort to encourage Mr. A to distinguish between "making a pass" and committing rape. The therapist suggested that Mr. A ask his female friends whether his asking an attractive woman out for coffee would be offensive, even if he did so bluntly. The fourth and final session began with Mr. A saying that a woman friend had responded to his inquiry about whether an attractive woman would find a coffee invitation offensive by saying, "I thought you'd never ask."

FOLLOW-UP

No follow-up information is available on Mr. A, although some comments on the use of the 16PF in regard to his case may be valuable. In brief treatment, we believe that the challenge is often to ensure that the limited time is not spent on irrelevancies or sidetracks. A presenting picture identical to Mr. A's could be associated with a much more disturbed or introverted or tough-minded young man. In such a case, the test findings would divert the clinical conversation onto a significantly different path from that taken with Mr. A. For example, if the young man's overall adjustment were questionable, the session probably would address his hidden expectations about romance. Perhaps under these hypothetical circumstances, his reluctance to approach women could be attributed to his needing much more from them than just a girlfriend relationship. Alternative hypotheses associated with poor overall adjustment might include his being in a fragmented state, needing help integrating desire and ego functions. Another hypothesis could be that a rejection would be too devastating. Alternative approaches could be developed for other potential personality types.

None of the preceding issues were raised by Mr. A's 16PF profile. In fact, his profile directed the way to the working hypothesis, which integrated Mr. A's moralizing, tender-mindedness, and ambivalence about lust.

CASE II: MR. B, AGE 28

REFERRAL

A police officer, Mr. B had been put on report for making comments in jest about shooting suspects because the courts were too lenient. In discussing the incidents with his captain, Mr. B revealed that he recently had married a prostitute whom he had met three months earlier while arresting her. Mr. B said that because his wife had expensive tastes, he was working a second job to support her. The captain referred Mr. B for a psychiatric evaluation, and the psychological testing was conducted as a consultation to the psychiatrist. On interview, the psychiatrist found a mild, situationally based anxiety disorder.

MR. B's 16PF PROFILE

PRIMARY TRAITS

Factor		Sten
A	Warmth	4
B	Reasoning	6
C	Ego Strength	3
E	Assertiveness	1
F	Liveliness	4
G	Rule-Consciousness	7
H	Social Boldness	5
I	Sensitivity	10
L	Vigilance	8
M	Impracticality	6
N	Privateness	6
O	Apprehension	9
Q1	Openness to Change	6
Q2	Self-Reliance	5
Q3	Compulsivity	4
Q4	Tension	7

RESPONSE SET SCORES

Scale		Percentile
IM	Impression Management	15
ACQ	Acquiescence	51
INF	Infrequency	47

GLOBAL FACTORS

Scale		Sten
EX	Extraversion	4.5
AX	Anxiety	9.2
TM	Tough-Mindedness	3.2
IN	Independence	3.3
SC	Self-Control	5.6

PROFILE INTERPRETATION

This is an extremely anxious (AX = 9.2) man with few inner coping resources (C = 3, Q3 = 4) to help him with his turmoil. He
also lacks readily available, significant social supports (EX = 4.5).
Problems are indicated in his ability to find suitable and satisfying
expressions of aggression (E = 1, IN = 3.3). Instead, his aggression tends to be released in socially isolating forms (L = 8). The
situational anxiety caused by his realization that his job is in jeop-
ardy and his struggle to make ends meet is probably raising his
scores somewhat on Apprehension (O = 9) and Tension (Q4 = 7),
but long-term adjustment problems also are indicated by his
coping deficits and aggression inhibitions.

To reveal so many problems in a fitness-for-duty evaluation is
unusual, and Mr. B's candidness matches his low percentile score
on Impression Management (IM = 15). On interview, he clearly
seemed interested in making a good impression and in gaining
sympathy for his financial straits. He may have viewed the 16PF
as an opportunity to publicize his suffering in an effort to be
forced out of his untenable position, whereas direct statements
on interview may have seemed a betrayal of his new wife and a
capitulation to his parents (who were very hostile to the marriage). His particularly passive efforts to find a solution are
probably very much in character (E = 1, I = 10, F = 4, H = 5).

Indeed, Mr. B's passivity may have gotten him into his current fix.
He reported becoming a police officer at his father's urging, and
the marked mismatch between him and his job indicates that he
has contorted himself rather badly to fulfill his father's wishes.
When marriage offered him an equally passive avenue that also
retaliated against his parents, he accepted. He chose a path in
opposition to his parents' wishes that was doomed to failure, fulfilling his self-expectations of the harm that would come to him if
he ever let them down. His earliest memory was of being late for
church the first time that he was to get there on his own; he was
scared in the churchyard by a large dog. This pattern of helpless-
ness and passivity when disappointing his parents fits his 16PF
profile very well. That he places importance on living up to his
parents' standards even though he has not internalized them into a
reliable identity structure is implied by the combination of Rule-
Consciousness (G+) and ineffective habits for binding anxiety (Q3-).

His parents seem to be playing a role of active disapproval of him, enabling him to resent them rather than engage in self-reproach. Suicide prevention should be considered because of his intense feelings of guilt (O = 9) and the general indication that he is overwhelmed (AX = 9.2). Further, his introversion and inhibitions around aggression raise questions about whether he has suitable outlets for his intense frustration. When people have firearms handy, they only have to be intensely suicidal for a minute or two for the results to be fatal. If Mr. B is recommended for medical leave, he should turn in his weapons. For him, suicide could be a self-enactment of the intense conflict he experiences among the following: doing the right thing, expressing anger poorly, and being a passive victim. Actually, his marriage may be a kind of suicide attempt, representing an effort to escape a situation that he did not feel allowed to escape.

FOLLOW-UP

Mr. B was put on medical leave, largely because of the testing results. He entered therapy and also received some financial counseling. His wife was arrested for shoplifting, and while she was incarcerated (for violating probation), the therapist did some shuttle diplomacy between Mr. B and his parents. The therapist suggested to the parents that if they were right about their son's marriage not lasting, they could afford to reconcile with him. After the wife had been released from jail, she did not adhere to the budget developed in therapy. Mr. B subsequently left her, not because of her history as a prostitute or his parents' wishes but because of irreconcilable differences concerning financial goals. Mr. B refused to contemplate any possibility of leaving the police force, and returned to duty about four months after the initial evaluation on the recommendation of the psychiatrist.

CASE III: MR. C, AGE 26

REFERRAL

Mr. C was tested in jail, where he had been for 16 months. He claimed that all his problems were the result of his alcoholism. He was suing for custody of his son who had been born 14 months earlier and had been put up for adoption by the mother,

Mr. C's ex-wife. She refused to testify against Mr. C, saying she was afraid of him.

On interview, this high school graduate was friendly and engaging, but he declared discussion of every third or fourth topic to be off-limits. This was understandable when the question related to criminal behaviors or things that might make him look bad, but he also refused to discuss why his father might have left the family when Mr. C was a baby and how he thought his son felt about visiting him in jail.

MR. C'S 16PF PROFILE

PRIMARY TRAITS

Factor		Sten
A	Warmth	7
B	Reasoning	5
C	Ego Strength	6
E	Assertiveness	8
F	Liveliness	8
G	Rule-Consciousness	8
H	Social Boldness	9
I	Sensitivity	1
L	Vigilance	6
M	Impracticality	3
N	Privateness	6
O	Apprehension	1
Q1	Openness to Change	4
Q2	Self-Reliance	9
Q3	Compulsivity	3
Q4	Tension	1

RESPONSE SET SCORES

Scale		Percentile
IM	Impression Management	97
ACQ	Acquiescence	51
INF	Infrequency	47

Global Factors

Scale		Sten
EX	Extraversion	6.2
AX	Anxiety	1.8
TM	Tough-Mindedness	9.0
IN	Independence	7.7
SC	Self-Control	5.7

Profile Interpretation

The combination of Mr. C being in jail and being a stranger to guilt (O = 1) immediately raises concerns about antisocial tendencies. His profile also offers some interesting contradictions. Although he tried to present a socially desirable impression of himself, he appears disorganized (Q3 = 3) and aggressive (IN = 7.7). He is extremely tough-minded (TM = 9.0) and a loner (Q2 = 9), but affable (A = 7) and outgoing (EX = 6.2). He claims to be very rule-conscious (G = 8), but denies feelings of guilt (O = 1). Integrating these with his behavior on interview, his extraversion would seem to be genuine, but is backed up with rage if the other person does not respond as he wishes or expects.

He cares what others think of him and, at least in the short run, he may be successful at gaining the approbation of others. If he fails to win others over, his behavior can degenerate quickly into antisocial modes of relating. His rule-consciousness (G = 8) does not seem well internalized, judging from his disorderliness (Q3 = 3), and he probably would act impulsively if his pride in his self-control were overridden by his pride in being seen as tough. He possesses a burgeoning energy (E+, F+, H+), which may not be responsive to any sense of obligation (O = 1) beyond his exaggerated sense of self-importance (E+, H+, L+, O-, Q2+). After engaging others, he may act quite impulsively in reestablishing his ego-inflation if others make him feel weak or unimportant. This does not prove that his wife is justified in being afraid of him, but that he has a wife who claims to fear him does fit his personality profile.

His utter denial of Apprehension (O = 1) and Tension (Q4 = 1) bodes poorly for his ability to benefit from therapy since therapy requires at least an implicit acknowledgment that something needs to change. The only thing that Mr. C is willing to change is his drinking, but even after 16 months of enforced sobriety, his denial, anger, and tough-mindedness are still very much in evidence. His incarceration is probably more related to sociopathy than to drinking.

Mr. C's affability, which typically conceals his ruthlessness, makes him likely to try to win over service providers and lure them into advocacy roles on his behalf. If they support his cause to gain custody of his son, they are likely to lose the leverage necessary to effect change. If they remain neutral and focus on helping him alter problematic behaviors, they are likely to lose his cooperation. If they become his advocates, they may not even realize, because of his genuine interpersonal skills, that they are doing so partly out of intimidation.

Mr. C's service plan must be written with care, since his determination probably would enable him to comply with the plan's demands without ever internalizing its purpose. He is quite capable of participating in therapy without being affected by it. Focus must be maintained on Mr. C's ability to anticipate, recognize, and meet his son's emotional and developmental needs—not on Mr. C's superficial behaviors. He is likely to be quite affectionate and playful when his son is behaving according to his plan. Therefore, key observations should focus on how Mr. C reacts when the boy is cranky or expresses his autonomy strivings in opposition to his father's desires.

FOLLOW-UP

Once he left jail, Mr. C made continual excuses for missing sessions with three consecutive therapists. Eventually, he found a therapist who believed his anger at the department of social services and at his ex-wife was justified. This therapist intended to testify on Mr. C's behalf, in spite of APA cautions about playing both therapeutic and evaluative roles in custody cases. Meanwhile, Mr. C was faced with the prospect of returning to jail, since he was being prosecuted for stalking his son's adoption worker, who had recommended that the boy be adopted by the foster parents. The 16PF was helpful in portraying Mr. C's criminal history as a logical extension of his personality, not as just a lapse that would not reflect on his ability to parent.

Case IV: Ms. D, Age 23

Referral

Ms. D sought therapy after her parents said she could no longer live rent free in an apartment they owned if she stayed married to her husband. She was supporting her husband by working two full-time jobs, neither of which related to her course of study in a two-year college. Denying that she was the victim of physical or emotional abuse by her spouse, she maintained that if she were the husband and he the homemaker, nobody would complain. She wanted the therapist to help her explain this to her parents.

Ms. D's 16PF Profile

Primary Traits

Factor		Sten
A	Warmth	5
B	Reasoning	5
C	Ego Strength	7
E	Assertiveness	6
F	Liveliness	5
G	Rule-Consciousness	8
H	Social Boldness	7
I	Sensitivity	5
L	Vigilance	3
M	Impracticality	2
N	Privateness	4
O	Apprehension	2
Q1	Openness to Change	5
Q2	Self-Reliance	2
Q3	Compulsivity	7
Q4	Tension	2

Response Set Scores

Scale		Percentile
IM	Impression Management	99
ACQ	Acquiescence	68
INF	Infrequency	51

GLOBAL FACTORS

Scale		Sten
EX	Extraversion	7.0
AX	Anxiety	1.3
TM	Tough-Mindedness	7.2
IN	Independence	5.6
SC	Self-Control	8.2

PROFILE INTERPRETATION

Ms. D tried to look her best on the testing (IM = 99), an impression that corresponded with her stated reason for seeking therapy. This presentation may have artificially lowered her score on global Anxiety (AX = 1.3); however, the anxiety-related primary factors (C, L, O, Q4) show no problem scores, and the high scores on Rule-Consciousness (G = 8) and Compulsivity (Q3 = 7) along with her Extraversion score (EX = 7.0) suggest a fairly healthy profile. The high IM score may reflect her understanding of social norms and her ability to manifest pursuit of her goals. Some masculine identification is evident in her tough-mindedness (TM = 7.2), which certainly fits the presenting complaint. In fact, the profile so closely fits Ms. D's argument that consideration could be given to inviting her parents to a session, if not for persuasion, then at least to discuss their daughter's point of view.

Another approach would be to question Ms. D's reliance on her parents, a childlike stance that is reiterated in her requesting professionals to represent her argument. This stance is indicated on her profile by her ingenuous frankness (N = 4), her low self-reliance (Q2 = 2), and her freedom from feelings of guilt (O = 2). Her stated goal, in fact, is to maintain her status as a tenant of her parents.

Her Self-Reliance score (Q2 = 2) is certainly unusual for a woman who is working two full-time jobs and who is trying to present well. In spite of possibly possessing a reservoir of inner resources, Ms. D may have an ideal image of how she is supposed to behave, one that emphasizes dependency and which was manifested via the testing when she tried to look her best. In conjunction with her intense persistence (SC = 8.2), this adherence to an image implies that she is unlikely to yield on her intention to support her husband. Even though her work would seem to put him in the dependent role, her own dependent posture indicates that she probably would continue to make sacrifices for the marriage.

Ms. D's low score on Apprehension (O = 2) raises questions about the fragility and superficiality of her rule-consciousness. Her ego strength (C = 7) and compulsivity (Q3 = 7) suggest that self-control has been successfully internalized. On occasion, she may justify impulsive behavior as being aligned with her belief system, and at those times, she may not feel answerable to parental introjects. The drama around the marriage may be an example of this.

The therapist may find that one meeting with Ms. D's husband would provide more insight into her psychology than lengthy assessments and ongoing treatment. Is he using drugs and exploiting her? Does she come home from the two jobs and then cook and clean? Or does he fulfill his end of the nontraditional arrangement?

FOLLOW-UP

The husband, who attended the second session, turned out to be a likable young man with no ambitions beyond raising a family and being a doting father. In fact, he and his wife were trying to start a family, and he intended to be the primary parent. Ms. D's parents persisted in their incomprehension of their daughter's and her husband's choices. Their disparagement of the husband continued, centered as much on his long hair and beard as on his lack of employment outside of the home. The therapist asked Ms. D what would happen if she simply ignored her parents' threats and their reservations about her husband. Ms. D acknowledged that her parents would never actually evict her. She also recognized that her and her husband's role reversal was merely serving as a focus for discontent that her parents would express in one way or another. The therapy concluded after three sessions, with the couple speculating that relations with Ms. D's parents would improve dramatically if a grandchild became a reality.

The 16PF results served to keep the focus on Ms. D's unusual presenting complaint. Her situation, as she described it, fit her personality and thus was accepted at face value. Further, the testing highlighted dependency issues that became intrinsic to the conversations.

CASE V: MR. E, AGE 23

REFERRAL

Mr. E was referred by his attorney, who requested an evaluation in regard to a sentencing recommendation. Mr. E had been arrested for groping a woman's breasts. The woman did not know Mr. E; she was merely walking by him on the street one night when he assaulted her. Later that same evening, Mr. E witnessed a different woman being pushed out of a car. Mr. E tried to comfort her and offered to drive her to a hospital. She refused his assistance, but he was so persistent that she called the police to report him, which is how he got caught for the first offense. Mr. E admitted the assault on the first woman, claiming drunkenness after imbibing eight mixed drinks in a short period of time; however, he denied any sexual or conscious intent of any kind.

Mr. E had been working as a waiter since finishing high school. He reported that all his spare time was spent watching TV, "whatever happens to be on."

MR. E'S 16PF PROFILE

PRIMARY TRAITS

Factor		Sten
A	Warmth	4
B	Reasoning	5
C	Ego Strength	6
E	Assertiveness	4
F	Liveliness	4
G	Rule-Consciousness	4
H	Social Boldness	3
I	Sensitivity	8
L	Vigilance	4
M	Impracticality	3
N	Privateness	5
O	Apprehension	6
Q1	Openness to Change	6
Q2	Self-Reliance	8
Q3	Compulsivity	6
Q4	Tension	8

RESPONSE SET SCORES

Scale		Percentile
IM	Impression Management	38
ACQ	Acquiescence	47
INF	Infrequency	78

GLOBAL FACTORS

Scale		Sten
EX	Extraversion	3.5
AX	Anxiety	6.0
TM	Tough-Mindedness	5.1
IN	Independence	3.7
SC	Self-Control	6.1

PROFILE INTERPRETATION

The combination of above-average global Anxiety (AX = 6.0) and below-average Extraversion (EX = 3.5) immediately creates an impression of the kind of person who may become a client since a dearth of both internal and external resources is indicated. Mr. E apparently has adequate ego strength (C = 6), but this asset is not being brought to bear on his problems with tension (Q4 = 8) and interpersonal relatedness. He is a timid (H = 3), sensitive (I = 8), anxious (Q4 = 8) young man with few social skills and little joy (F = 4) in life. His subdued passivity (IN = 3.7) does not ensconce him pleasantly among his peers (EX = 3.5), and likely causes him to endure occasional eruptions of resentment. His offense may have been an amalgam of psychological motives; that is, an attempt to reach out to a woman in his loneliness, to express pent-up frustrated aggressions, and to reinforce or justify his avoidant and resentful stance by inspiring rebuff.

Judging from Mr. E's profile, incarceration would do him little good. A jail sentence likely would cost him his job—his one anchor to self-esteem and a mainstream adjustment—and probably make him even more isolated and resentful. A more effective punishment might involve his tithing to women's shelters as a general restitution. If such is recommended, it should be anonymous so that it does not become a twisted effort at helping that encroaches on the women's personal space, analogous to the second incident the night of Mr. E's arrest. This kind of restitution should depend on a probation that excludes all alcohol consumption. Whatever the reasons for his drinking, Mr. E's use of alcohol may be a likely antecedent for his criminal behavior.

In addition to facing any consequences that society demands, Mr. E needs to learn some positive social skills. His score on Rule-Consciousness (G = 4) is not extraordinarily low, but in conjunction with his behavior, it raises concerns about whether he is aware of how people conduct interpersonal business in our society.*

*In a moment of lucidity and insight, a schizophrenic man with a Rule-Consciousness score of 1 admitted to one of us that he did not know the "code" that people use in our society. "I'm not being paranoid," he said. "There is a code. Somehow, when a guy buys a beer at a bar and points at the game on the TV and says to the guy next to him, 'What's the score?' they both know the code that lets the other guy know the first guy is OK. When I say it, the other guy just grunts at me and looks uncomfortable."

Obviously, Mr. E knows that grabbing a stranger's breasts is not likely to lead to romance, but he does not seem to know the instrumental acts that could lead to a romance. Milton Erickson helped a young man similar to Mr. E (though less impulsive) by inducing him to take ballroom dancing lessons, assuming that eventually he would come across an equally timid and unskilled, yet hopeful, young woman. The idea would be to help Mr. E apply some of the strengths (C = 6, B = 5, Q3 = 6) that have helped him maintain a job to the problems of his social life.

FOLLOW-UP

Mr. E's attorney thought the psychological report, of which the 16PF profile was only a part, raised too many issues. He believed that the report could lead to a longer probation than Mr. E was likely to get without it. The lawyer had hoped that the report would portray Mr. E as a healthy young man with a drinking problem. Since Mr. E was not considered by the court to be sexually dangerous, he was given a year's probation with a requirement of attending either counseling or AA for three months. Mr. E chose AA, possibly because it was gratis.

CASE VI: MR. F, AGE 35

REFERRAL

A self-employed plumber and a karate instructor, Mr. F was seen in an effort to help settle a custody dispute. His wife had left him for his best friend 6 years earlier, and ever since, he had been seeing his son every other weekend. The son, now age 7, called the police to report that the stepfather had threatened him with a gun. The police believed the boy's story over that of the mother and stepfather, and placed him with Mr. F, who petitioned the court to keep him.

MR. F'S 16PF PROFILE

PRIMARY TRAITS

Factor		Sten
A	Warmth	1
B	Reasoning	5
C	Ego Strength	8
E	Assertiveness	4
F	Liveliness	4
G	Rule-Consciousness	6
H	Social Boldness	6
I	Sensitivity	4
L	Vigilance	5
M	Impracticality	5
N	Privateness	2
O	Apprehension	7
Q1	Openness to Change	3
Q2	Self-Reliance	8
Q3	Compulsivity	9
Q4	Tension	3

RESPONSE SET SCORES

Scale		Percentile
IM	Impression Management	68
ACQ	Acquiescence	52
INF	Infrequency	68

GLOBAL FACTORS

Scale		Sten
EX	Extraversion	4.1
AX	Anxiety	3.9
TM	Tough-Mindedness	8.6
IN	Independence	3.9
SC	Self-Control	7.5

PROFILE INTERPRETATION

Mr. F is extremely reserved (A = 1), especially in regard to
emotional exchanges with other people (TM = 8.6, I = 4);
however, a schizoid withdrawal is unlikely in consideration of his
Ego Strength score (C = 8), even if it was elevated somewhat by
an understandable effort to look good under the circumstances.
That effort must not have been too pervasive since he scored only
at the 68th percentile on Impression Management. Perhaps he is
so socially aloof that he does not understand what is considered
socially desirable behavior, although his psychosocial history and
some of the positive features of his profile (C = 8, G = 6, Q3 = 9,
AX = 3.9, SC = 7.5) suggest otherwise. His emotional coldness
may indicate that encountering rejection (e.g., his wife leaving
him for his best friend) is a familiar experience for him. He may
not reflect enough warmth back into relationships to sustain them
because a history of rejection makes him cautious and his lack of
warmth then culminates in his being ignored and rejected yet
again. He may rely on his masculine identification (e.g., tough-
mindedness, karate) to achieve a method of not being ignored and
pushed aside so easily.

Finding so much Ego Strength (C = 8) and Compulsivity (Q3 = 9)
in someone so inhibited (E = 4, F = 4, IN = 3.9) is unusual. Mr.
F appears to have a wealth of controls, many more than are
needed. The unusual combination of Apprehension (O = 7) and
low Tension (Q4 = 3) reinforces this picture, as if he is saying that
he guards himself regularly but does not become impatient or
tense frequently enough to warrant using the controls. This
pattern fits the hypothesis that a history of rejection has made
him extremely cautious interpersonally and that his hesitance
eventually confirms his fears by distancing others.

Mr. F's self-employment as a plumber fits his emotional isolation,
his compulsivity, his unaggressiveness, and his masculine identification. Taking his son into the trade with him, or at least taking
him along on some of his jobs, could be a way of offering some
bonds to the boy without overly challenging Mr. F's emotional
reservations. Involving his son in karate could achieve the same
end.

Mr. F's profile does not raise custody concerns that would normally warrant state oversight. The child will need to maintain a relationship with his mother and possibly with other sources of nurturance as well. Managing the ensuing loyalty issues smoothly may be difficult for Mr. F (as for any father). A therapist for the boy might get involved briefly to help with the transition and to consult with Mr. F about the child's adjustment to his new home. One agenda item for this consultation might be to help Mr. F appreciate the permanency of his relationship with his son, so that in spite of temporary setbacks and retreats, Mr. F can try to minimize his self-protective emotional withdrawal when dealing with the child.

FOLLOW-UP

The mother is still married to the stepfather, but he leaves their home whenever the child visits. The mother's loyalty to this man has never been addressed as a psychological issue for the boy. The child never speaks to one parent about the other. He showed no adjustment symptoms during the transition, and therapy was discontinued. Mr. F takes the boy on as many emergency calls as possible and practical, and the child has become an avid karate enthusiast.

CASE VII: MS. G, AGE 43

REFERRAL

After years of being battered, Ms. G fled from the home with her 8-year-old son in fear for her life. She refused to press charges against her husband or enter a shelter. Since no other family members could accommodate her and the child, she returned home; her son was placed in foster care. Ms. G's explanation was that as bad as her husband was, he did treat her better than her father had treated her mother. Her father had abused her mother, and one day, threw her out of the house. Ms. G, who was 15 at the time, stayed with her father as did her younger sister. Her mother died about a year later of physical complications from the abuse.

The state requested a psychological evaluation of Ms. G prior to deciding whether to let the child return home; however, the state's position almost certainly would be to keep the child in foster care. The father refused to participate in any services or assessments.

Ms. G's 16PF Profile

Primary Traits

Factor		Sten
A	Warmth	8
B	Reasoning	2
C	Ego Strength	3
E	Assertiveness	2
F	Liveliness	1
G	Rule-Consciousness	5
H	Social Boldness	3
I	Sensitivity	7
L	Vigilance	6
M	Impracticality	2
N	Privateness	7
O	Apprehension	8
Q1	Openness to Change	6
Q2	Self-Reliance	7
Q3	Compulsivity	5
Q4	Tension	6

Response Set Scores

Scale		Percentile
IM	Impression Management	24
ACQ	Acquiescence	65
INF	Infrequency	88

Global Factors

Scale		Sten
EX	Extraversion	3.5
AX	Anxiety	7.8
TM	Tough-Mindedness	5.1
IN	Independence	2.9
SC	Self-Control	7.0

PROFILE INTERPRETATION

The Infrequency scale is slightly elevated (the question mark alternative was selected for five items as opposed to the usual zero or one), and Impression Management is a bit low (IM = 24). Ms. G's test-taking attitude reflects signs of the indecision, passivity, and self-hate that dominate her personality profile. Her passivity—her sense that things happen to her, not because of her—is evident in her low Ego Strength (C = 3), submissiveness (E = 2), lack of energy (F = 1), and timidity (H = 3). Even her low score on Reasoning (B = 2), which is probably a result of concentration problems (C-, O+), suggests passivity. She cannot attain even the score one would expect from guessing. Her dissipated cognitive resources leave her ill-prepared to meet life's challenges proactively and further exacerbate her passive stance.

The combination of global Anxiety (AX = 7.8) and introversion (EX = 3.5) raises questions about internal resources and external supports. This pattern is often seen in people who become clients, especially when Ego Strength (C = 3) is also low. In Ms. G's case, the problems in functioning are expressed more in a dependency stance toward her husband than toward the mental health system (as would be expected in a client). Indeed, her entire personality profile can be seen as an adaptation to the violent behavior of the men in her life—first her father and then her husband. She tries to "lie low" (E-, F-, H-) so as not to attract the man's attention. She maintains her self-control (SC = 7.0) to avoid the man's harsh attacks. The stress and fear are kept inside (O = 8) with few if any suitable outlets for her aggression (IN = 2.9). She substituted her husband for her father to make sense of her identity, and if she left her husband, she might have to find a violent substitute for him as well.

The one score in this profile that does not fit Ms. G's adaptation to her father or husband is the 8 on Warmth (A). Her psychosocial history confirms that she is socially isolated and has never had a real friend besides her little sister; yet she perceives herself as interested in and familiar with warm emotional exchanges with others. Her interest in dependency exchanges may suggest a desperate search for help, or it may reflect her self-perception as a caregiver who did as much as she could for her mother and sister. If so, this self-perception may provide the opportunity to extract her from her current situation; her concern for her son may impel her to leave her current situation for good. She grew up in a holocaust from which there was no escape, and expressed her caring by huddling with her sister. This method of showing concern is only appropriate in situations where escape is impossible. She has not yet absorbed the idea that she is not a child in her current family, and that unlike her family of origin, she may be able to leave it (although it might take some doing in light of her husband's threats).

In all likelihood the state cannot condone returning a child to such a violent home as this one is assumed to be. Communicating to Ms. G that she is a bad mother for not protecting her son is pointless since this would only make her think worse of herself and make her even more vulnerable to her husband's reported efforts to control her. Instead, the probable decision to keep the child in foster care could be presented as a favor to her, a way to keep her boy safe until she can find the strength to do so herself. She might acknowledge that she would have felt very lonely if her little sister had been removed from their childhood home but that she also would have been glad for her sister to escape.

FOLLOW-UP

The husband stalked the child in the foster home, even after a restraining order was obtained by the state. The district attorney's office successfully pressed for the husband's incarceration. While he was locked up, evidence of other serious crimes emerged, and he went to prison. Ms. G moved to a different city, where she was reunited with her son. She soon developed a drinking problem, conceptualized by the family therapist as yet another way of organizing around a violent force that kept her vulnerable, dependent, and distraught. As her husband was an improved version of her father, John Barleycorn was an improved version of her husband. Although Ms. G could not envision herself in the battered women's network, many aspects of AA did appeal to her, including the emphases on becoming a helper of others and on practicing humility as opposed to empowerment. She obtained minimum-wage employment and became active in AA. In addition, she spent a lot of time trying to help her son overcome adjustment problems.

Case VIII: Ms. H, Age 28

Referral

The state placed Ms. H's three children in foster care based on reports from daycare providers of poor hygiene and other signs of neglect. Ms. H's service plan for regaining custody of her children included a psychological evaluation. She denied any problems in her family of origin, but acknowledged that she had been sexually abused by her father's brother when she was 7 years old. At the time, no charges were pressed because "we didn't want our name dragged through the mud."

She has been working in a factory since her children were removed; before that, she was on welfare. She was openly hostile to the psychologist and refused to answer many questions.

Ms. H's 16PF Profile

Primary Traits

Factor		Sten
A	Warmth	6
B	Reasoning	6
C	Ego Strength	4
E	Assertiveness	6
F	Liveliness	4
G	Rule-Consciousness	6
H	Social Boldness	2
I	Sensitivity	7
L	Vigilance	10
M	Impracticality	3
N	Privateness	9
O	Apprehension	9
Q1	Openness to Change	5
Q2	Self-Reliance	9
Q3	Compulsivity	7
Q4	Tension	8

RESPONSE SET SCORES

Scale		Percentile
IM	Impression Management	24
ACQ	Acquiescence	83
INF	Infrequency	95

GLOBAL FACTORS

Scale		Sten
EX	Extraversion	2.4
AX	Anxiety	9.8
TM	Tough-Mindedness	5.7
IN	Independence	5.5
SC	Self-Control	7.3

PROFILE INTERPRETATION

Ms. H is a timid (H = 2) and angry (L = 10) loner (Q2 = 9) whose defenses are not working (O+, Q4+). Her overall psychological adjustment may be impaired, judging from her global Anxiety (AX = 9.8), low Ego Strength (C = 4), and numerous problem scores. She seems to have some capacity to adopt a functional persona (B = 6, G = 6, N = 9, Q3 = 7), but this likely would be used in the service of hiding herself from others rather than for garnering social reinforcers (EX = 2.4).

The children's poor hygiene may reflect patterns from her childhood. For example, consider her striking comment that the pressing of charges against her childhood abuser, not the sexual abuse itself, would have dragged the family name through the mud. Her parents' reported reaction to the abuse indicates neglect of the child's needs. Ms. H's idealization of her parents, at her own expense, leaves her very angry at them and all that they represent; however, she cannot experience this anger directly without ruining the idealization that she depends on to justify her own neglect. Her neglect of her children thus serves several psychological purposes: (1) reinforces the family pattern of avoiding children's needs, (2) enables her to thumb her nose at her parents by involving her with child welfare agencies, and (3) allows her to vent her anger at the state, thus sparing the parents she still needs to idealize.

Ms. H's paranoia probably has been exacerbated by recent events. Having the state call her a "bad mother" may have stimulated fears about her adequacy as a woman. She seems to be blaming her children's placement in foster care on a conspiracy theory rather than taking responsibility for their poor hygiene. For example, because the Daycare providers merely stated that her children were arriving "filthy," she inspected them only for dirt. She claims that the complaint should have specified instead that the kids smelled like urine so she could have checked them for the odor. She did stop short of claiming that the Daycare facility had committed this "error" on purpose. Still, she blamed the Daycare personnel's word choice rather than her own parenting for the children smelling like urine.

Psychotherapy, psychotropic medication for intense anxiety, and parent skills training are all appropriate services, but are unlikely to help. Judging from Ms. H's reaction to the assessment, she maintains a hostile relationship with people assigned to oversee her parenting functioning, and this attitude is likely to extend to any service provider who tries to help her improve. She has a tremendous amount of personal investment in the idea that children must fend for themselves, which enables her to maintain her idealization of her parents. Indeed, the concept of improving as a parent is as foreign to her as the notion that her parents might have assumed responsibility for what happened to her.

FOLLOW-UP

Ms. H regularly missed visits with her children, and she refused any involvement with the mental health system. Her parent-skills trainer cleaned her house, and Ms. H was able to maintain it fairly well, at least while the children were away. The state began to pursue adoption proceedings, which Ms. H was contesting in court.

CASE IX: MS. J, AGE 27

REFERRAL

Her physician sent this college graduate for therapy when he learned that she was carrying the 50 Valium he had prescribed for her in a coat pocket. The pills were stuck together in a lump, and whenever Ms. J felt anxious, she would take out the lump and lick it. She refused to be evaluated by a woman psychologist.

Ms. J is not and has never been married. She explained that she calls herself a "housewife" because she keeps her own house, not a husband's. Her earliest memory is of walking for the first time. Her mother had refused to buy her a treat from the ice cream truck. The truck was pulling away so she got up and walked after it.

MS. J'S 16PF PROFILE

PRIMARY TRAITS

Factor		Sten
A	Warmth	5
B	Reasoning	4
C	Ego Strength	1
E	Assertiveness	8
F	Liveliness	7
G	Rule-Consciousness	2
H	Social Boldness	5
I	Sensitivity	4
L	Vigilance	10
M	Impracticality	7
N	Privateness	4
O	Apprehension	9
Q1	Openness to Change	9
Q2	Self-Reliance	9
Q3	Compulsivity	4
Q4	Tension	9

RESPONSE SET SCORES

Scale		Percentile
IM	Impression Management	5
ACQ	Acquiescence	93
INF	Infrequency	99

GLOBAL FACTORS

Scale		Sten
EX	Extraversion	5.1
AX	Anxiety	10.0
TM	Tough-Mindedness	4.2
IN	Independence	8.8
SC	Self-Control	2.7

PROFILE INTERPRETATION

The presenting problem immediately raises concerns about psychosis, and Ms. J's profile does little to assuage those concerns. The validity scales suggest some distortion since all are deviant. A low opinion of herself may have lowered her Impression Management score, but another possibility is that this scale (having 11 of 12 items keyed toward the c response alternative) merely picked up a bizarre preference for the a response choice (which weighs ACQ) and the b choice (which weighs INF). The profile might be declared invalid except for the fact that she endorsed so many of the global Anxiety items, actually scoring 11.5 on a 10-point scale. Faking bad is a possibility since IM is so low. In the context of a presumed paranoid psychosis and her refusal to see a woman psychologist, one hypothesis is that Ms. J believes the male intake worker will remain in her life if she performs poorly on the testing.

This paranoid woman is currently overwhelmed, and she is extremely prone to angry (L = 10, IN = 8.8) outbursts (SC = 2.7). Her Valium-licking behavior may represent an effort to deflect her rage with a sexualized dependency on her doctor (thus the question of whether she has a crush on the intake worker). The pattern in Ms. J's earliest memory suggests that the ice-cream man is unattainable, and although more literal than most of our interpretations of early memories, she may have substituted the doctor for the ice-cream man. Her earliest memory also shows her engaging in independent behavior (walking) to defend against feelings of maternal deprivation. This consideration suggests that a long-term therapy relationship with a woman might create a vessel for positive maternal transactions, although Ms. J may be too embedded in her aversion to women to accept such a relationship.

Ms. J can be quite forceful at times (IN = 8.8, E = 8, F = 7) in her pursuit of new experiences (Q1 = 9). Her forcefulness may have led the family doctor to prescribe Valium in the first place. This outlet for self-expression may be keeping her from deteriorating into a more fragmented psychosis; therefore, efforts to limit her "wild" behavior, as she calls it, should be undertaken cautiously. She would not say exactly what constitutes her wild behavior, but the pattern of paranoia, aversion to rules (G-), and assertive liveliness (E+, F+) reinforces the clinical impression of sexual conquest.

FOLLOW-UP

The clinic psychiatrist prescribed Stelazine, which helped eliminate blatant psychotic symptoms. Ms. J would only accept therapy with a male therapist, and the regular sessions appeared to contain her and keep her organized. In this case, appearances were deceiving, since after a few months of therapy, it became clear that it was therapy only to the therapist. Ms. J revealed that, in her mind, she and her therapist had been dating regularly and that having a steady "beau" had reduced her "wildness." The therapist decided to work with this psychotic belief rather than dispel it. (He did tell her it was not true, but did not press the point when she replied that she knew he had to say that.) In addition, the therapist arranged for intensive supervision out of concern for potential liability issues.

CASE X: MS. K, AGE 32

REFERRAL

A high school graduate who was working as a receptionist, Ms. K was a victim of sexual abuse, having been repeatedly raped by a male cousin throughout her childhood. Her mother had never believed Ms. K's accusations, and her father had not been involved with the family for years. Ms. K came in for therapy when she started having nightmares and flashbacks, which were stimulated by her making plans to marry.

Ms. K's 16PF Profile

Primary Traits

Factor		Sten
A	Warmth	8
B	Reasoning	3
C	Ego Strength	3
E	Assertiveness	4
F	Liveliness	3
G	Rule-Consciousness	6
H	Social Boldness	3
I	Sensitivity	4
L	Vigilance	6
M	Impracticality	2
N	Privateness	7
O	Apprehension	8
Q1	Openness to Change	7
Q2	Self-Reliance	8
Q3	Compulsivity	4
Q4	Tension	6

Response Set Scores

Scale		Percentile
IM	Impression Management	5
ACQ	Acquiescence	65
INF	Infrequency	93

Global Factors

Scale		Sten
EX	Extraversion	3.8
AX	Anxiety	7.8
TM	Tough-Mindedness	6.1
IN	Independence	4.4
SC	Self-Control	6.6

PROFILE INTERPRETATION

Concentration problems (C-, O+) probably account for Ms. K's high Infrequency score; she may have selected the question-mark alternative in favor of focusing on the items. The same inference may be made in relation to her performance on the Reasoning (B) items. Some information about her adjustment prior to developing her current symptoms would be helpful, although the brief referral information suggests that she was previously better defended against the effects of her sexual abuse.

Ms. K currently exhibits excessive turmoil (AX = 7.8, O = 8) with few coping skills (C = 3, B = 3, Q3 = 4) and few social skills (EX = 3.8). To some extent her turmoil is a reaction to, not a cause of, her flashbacks, but her lack of psychological resources cannot be explained away. She seems to have identity problems, in the sense that most people with a coherent self-experience find disorder less acceptable than she does (Q3 = 4). Her tough-mindedness (TM = 6.1, I = 4) and her practicality (M = 2) are unusual in someone this warm (A = 8), and make her more androgynous than someone with her limited ego strength usually can afford to be. In terms of identity integration, she might have been better off specializing in some version of womanliness, except that the sexual abuse may well have poisoned a feminine stance for her.

A "mother-who-does-not-believe-you" translates psychologically into an absence of support around self-expressions as well as feelings of insecurity. The psychology of Ms. K's perception of her mother's response to the abuse is reflected in her passivity and inhibitions around self-expression (E-, F-, H-). Ms. K may feel that even having a self at all puts her at risk of abuse, a fear that is not soothed by caring parental introjects. She may have experienced the abuse itself as a punishment for something she did or for an exuberant or optimistic way of being in the world that she now avoids.

The characterological issues implied by this interpretation suggest that brief treatment will not get at the problem. Conceptualizing this as a sex therapy case probably would be a mistake; such a hypothesis would assume that the prospect of a sexual relationship with her fiancé is stirring up sexual abuse issues from her childhood. Instead, identity problems and entrenched passivity suggest that the problem has less to do with sex and more to do with defining herself as a wife (i.e., as a family member). Ms. K may have used her Self-Reliance (Q2 = 8) and her Warmth (A = 8) to achieve a gregarious but impersonal adjustment to meet her affiliative needs without involvement in the kinds of familial relationships that she finds toxic. Now, the prospect of marriage may be disrupting that adjustment. She may have to process difficult and painful experiences from her childhood in long-term therapy before she will be able to function effectively in the familial role of "wife," a role that is loaded for her with expectations of abuse and neglect.

FOLLOW-UP

Ms. K accepted a referral for long-term therapy with a private practitioner (M.S.W.) who charges affordable rates and does not have to involve a managed care company. The confidentiality and the potential for the relationship to become a fixture in her life should facilitate the use of therapy as a reservoir (or a crucible) for her developmental problems. This should ease the pressure she feels about possibly losing her true self when and if her external world becomes too discordant with her inner world. The therapy will provide a reality check that the person she grew up being has not disappeared. Meanwhile, the therapy also can provide a vessel for changing that self.

CASE XI: MR. AND MRS. L, BOTH AGE 51

REFERRAL

This well-adjusted, middle-class, churchgoing couple was referred for family therapy by the department of social services. Mr. L was a factory foreman and farmer, and Mrs. L was a housewife and farmer. Their two sons were both in prison, one for armed robbery and the other for rape. Their grandson, the son of the armed robber, had been in their custody since birth. He was now 8, and had become a discipline problem at school. He also had been seen trying to kill birds with a sling shot. Mr. and Mrs. L had only one kind of explanation for all this misconduct.

Concerning the armed robber, they said, "He never settled down." Concerning their other son, they said, "He was always rambunctious." They recognized the severity of rape, but denied he had committed it, insisting he had just chosen to get involved with a vindictive young woman. About their grandson Bobby, they said, "Boys will be boys." Mr. L added, "We were probably worse than he is when we were coming up, but in those days you didn't make such a big deal about it."

16PF PROFILES FOR MR. AND MRS. L

PRIMARY TRAITS

Factor		Sten/Mr. L	Sten/Mrs. L
A	Warmth	3	8
B	Reasoning	5	3
C	Ego Strength	6	7
E	Assertiveness	8	2
F	Liveliness	6	2
G	Rule-Consciousness	8	8
H	Social Boldness	5	6
I	Sensitivity	7	5
L	Vigilance	5	6
M	Impracticality	6	3
N	Privateness	8	7
O	Apprehension	4	7
Q1	Openness to Change	9	3
Q2	Self-Reliance	8	3
Q3	Compulsivity	6	7
Q4	Tension	5	4

RESPONSE SET SCORES

Scale		Percentile/Mr. L	Percentile/Mrs. L
IM	Impression Management	57	72
ACQ	Acquiescence	47	37
INF	Infrequency	51	84

GLOBAL FACTORS

Scale		Sten/Mr. L	Sten/Mrs. L
EX	Extraversion	3.3	5.6
AX	Anxiety	4.3	5.0
TM	Tough-Mindedness	3.4	7.3
IN	Independence	7.8	2.9
SC	Self-Control	6.4	8.5

PROFILE INTERPRETATIONS

Mr. L's validity scales are within expected limits, indicating that he was as unaffectedly honest on the 16PF as he seemed to be on interview. The profile offers no reason to question his presentation as a well-adjusted individual. There are no problem scores, and he shows good Ego Strength (C = 6) and Self-Control (SC = 6.4). Global Anxiety was fairly low (4.3), and coupled with an average Impression Management score (57), may be another reliable indicator of overall adjustment.

Mr. L's adventurousness (Q1 = 9) does not seem to be expressed socially (H = 5, EX = 3.3) but in a quest for novel experiences. His assertiveness (E = 8) may lead him to set an agenda around getting his needs met, which others are then expected to honor. He may tend to disguise his needs by presenting the agenda in the form of rules (G = 8), leading to complicated interactions that hinder others from opting for their choices without making him feel slighted. His tendency to disguise his needs would be compounded by his privateness (N = 8); that is, he certainly has needs (I = 7), but since he prefers not to seem needy, he expresses these needs only as rules to be obeyed.

Mr. L may not have a lot to offer others emotionally (A = 3). He may see himself as a breadwinner who gives primarily by providing food and shelter. Having discharged his responsibilities by wage-earning, he then may feel free to indulge his interests (Q1 = 9). This makes for a rather superficial definition of obligation, which may be reflected in the differential between his scores on Rule-Consciousness (G = 8) and Apprehension (O = 4). For him, rules may not represent internalized guideposts as much as tasks that must be obeyed before being free to play, like eating vegetables before dessert.

Mrs. L's profile also provides little reason to question her presentation as well-adjusted. Although she is certainly very passive (E-, F-) and dependent (A+, E-, Q2-), these traits are balanced by Ego Strength (C = 7), average Extraversion (5.6), and good controls (SC = 8.5, Q3 = 7). She is tough-minded (I = 5) and practical (M = 3), very much the farmer's wife who is more concerned about getting the peas harvested than about all the nonsense with Bobby. Her version of womanhood is not traditionally feminine (TM = 7.3) in the connotation of sensitivity and histrionic dynamics, but it may be hyper-traditional in the sense of passivity and avoidance of aggression (IN = 2.9).

In the context of her passivity, Mrs. L's warmth (A = 8) may reflect the extent to which she gets her dependency needs met on both sides of the nurturance encounter (i.e., by giving as well as by receiving). Her extraversion is reportedly expressed in her immediate and extended families and through the church, which suggests how it is possible to be very warm and yet subdued by putting generosity into the service of other people's needs. Her warmth, passivity, rule-consciousness, privateness, resistance to change, group-dependency, and compulsivity add up to a desire to be a good girl, even at age 51.

Both Mr. and Mrs. L show well-organized social personas (G+, N+, Q3+) and ego strength (C+). Mr. L is more reserved (A-), assertive (E+), lively (F+), free from guilt (O-), experimenting (Q1+), and self-reliant (Q2+) than his wife. In spite of his Sensitivity (I = 7) (or because of it and to mask it), his presentation is that of a rugged individualist. His dynamics have him establishing the agenda as a set of rules; her dynamics have her following the agenda although it may allow too little room for her aggression. This may be all well and good as far as she is concerned, for she does not seem to miss her aggression. On the other hand, the power differential in their relationship may present a skewed impression of what it means to be male and female. Consequently, their sons and grandson may have come to define as female whatever is obedient, dependent, and nice, leaving to the male realm the alternatives of self-defining, independent, and naughty.

What for Mr. and Mrs. L is a settled and gratifying mode of relating may have become for their children a rigid system that put them in untenable states. Mr. and Mrs. L have enough ego strength to survive in the little world of "Captain and Cook" they have created, whereas their mode of exchange defined their sons and is in the process of defining Bobby. The implication may be that Bobby needs some exposure in family therapy to the fact that Mr. and Mrs. L's dominance hierarchy is a mutually defined agreement as opposed to the limited array of roles it seemingly represents. A boy having to choose between these two apparent extremes will choose to be the boss; this produces adjustment problems, but is better than the alternative as far as the child can determine. Another agenda for family therapy would be to open the question of whether Mr. and Mrs. L may be so involved with their chores, jobs, community responsibilities, and marital dynamics that they have little time and energy left over for parenting. Mr. and Mrs. L have parented, and are continuing to parent, high-maintenance children, who may be competing with their parents' other interests for their attention.

FOLLOW-UP

As predicted by the lack of discomfort in their 16PF profiles, Mr. and Mrs. L were affable and enthusiastic consumers of family therapy, but they had no intention of changing and saw no need to do so. Something of an amateur Will Rogers, Mr. L told many amusing anecdotes in therapy, while Mrs. L brought baked goods or garden vegetables to most sessions (and apologized when she did not). Bobby was involved in individual therapy and then in an after-school group, without showing any improvement. A Ritalin trial had equivocal effects since whether he actually received the medication was never clear. Residential treatment was under discussion, but Mr. and Mrs. L wanted to wait to see if his father's release from prison would have a positive effect on Bobby.

CASE XII: MS. M, AGE 27

REFERRAL

This African American woman lived in the inner city and worked full-time in a clerical position at a bank. A single parent, she was raising a 10-year-old daughter and had recently assumed custody of her 5-year-old nephew when her sister was jailed on drug charges. The nephew, who was on Ritalin, told his therapist that the daughter hit him with a belt whenever Ms. M left them alone and that Ms. M's boyfriend had molested him repeatedly in the park. Ms. M stated that both charges were beyond belief. She agreed to participate in a family assessment of which the 16PF was a component.

MS. M'S 16PF PROFILE

PRIMARY TRAITS

Factor		Sten
A	Warmth	7
B	Reasoning	6
C	Ego Strength	6
E	Assertiveness	4
F	Liveliness	6
G	Rule-Consciousness	9
H	Social Boldness	7
I	Sensitivity	7
L	Vigilance	4
M	Impracticality	3
N	Privateness	7
O	Apprehension	5
Q1	Openness to Change	5
Q2	Self-Reliance	6
Q3	Compulsivity	8
Q4	Tension	1

Response Set Scores

Scale		Percentile
IM	Impression Management	57
ACQ	Acquiescence	42
INF	Infrequency	51

Global Factors

Scale		Sten
EX	Extraversion	5.8
AX	Anxiety	2.8
TM	Tough-Mindedness	5.5
IN	Independence	4.6
SC	Self-Control	8.5

Profile Interpretation

Several features in Ms. M's profile suggest an essentially healthy personality. Her global Anxiety (AX = 2.8) is very low, and it apparently does not reflect an effort to exaggerate her socially desirable features (IM = 57). No problem scores were obtained; in other words, no areas of functioning are indicated that in and of themselves would raise questions about her overall adjustment. According to her Extraversion score (EX = 5.8), she is interpersonally connected and engaged. Her psychosocial history supports this impression, as she has proactively demonstrated her ability to function in the major life spheres. Of course, the 16PF may only be reflecting the same impersonal, social strengths that she manifests on interview, and perhaps another assessment of her more private functioning would reveal some significant problems. This is especially of concern when Rule-Consciousness (G), Privateness (N), and Compulsivity (Q3) are all high, as they are for Ms. M. These scales normally are the primary markers of an "as-if" or "false self" adjustment; however, the chance of Ms. M having this adjustment seems to be negated by her levels of Warmth (A = 7) and Ego Strength (C = 6). Still, other testing and the family interactions should be examined with this hypothesis in mind. (In fact, subsequent projective testing raised no concerns, and Ms. M's interactions with the boy were observed as being playful, respectful, and most importantly, tailored to and continuously responsive to signals from the child. The child's slurred and rapid speech was very difficult to understand unless Ms. M was in the room, and reportedly this was also the situation at school. Our hypothesis was that in her presence, the boy expects to be listened to and speaks accordingly.)

If Ms. M's excessive Self-Control (SC = 8.5) is not in the service of insulating a diffuse identity from contact with others, what is its purpose? Her scores on Independence (IN = 4.6) and Assertiveness (E = 4) are low, but not so low as to suggest problems with hostility that would need to be shielded from public scrutiny. She is certainly not the angry, impulsive type of person who would need excessive self-control just to function. Perhaps to be healthy and live in an inner city requires some supplementary defensive maneuvers. She is not shy, retiring, and avoidant, nor does she maintain an angry stance of self-protection. Instead, she is unusually careful, practical, and precise, perhaps because she deliberately idealizes and utilizes the virtues that put her on a different path from her sister.

Throughout the assessment, Ms. M was convinced that her nephew's accusations would be disproved. Her faith in the system was likely an extension of her faith in rules and her careful obedience to them. Undoubtedly, this faith has been repeatedly challenged by her life circumstances, but it also has been repeatedly strengthened by the self-esteem, money, and control that it has garnered for her by making her such a good worker. Her devotion to ethical behavior provides some insight into why she would risk unbalancing a fulfilling life by welcoming her nephew into it, a boy who is sure to have been through some significant social traumas.

The implication of the assessment on the referral question is that the relationship between the child and Ms. M should be protected as much as possible. While no individual's personal judgment can obviate the need to investigate allegations of abuse, Ms. M's assessment of her daughter's and boyfriend's behaviors should be taken seriously. She was amenable to the idea that answers were worth pursuing, especially when the determination was made to center the investigation on why the boy would make such accusations rather than solely on what the daughter and boyfriend had possibly done.

FOLLOW-UP

Ms. M explained to her nephew that he could remain with her in spite of all the trouble his accusations had caused. He never recanted his statements, but he did stop accusing. Moreover, he never showed any detectable anxiety or ambivalence about spending time alone with either the daughter or the boyfriend, although he was quite ambivalent about both in the family sessions. The family therapist hypothesized that because the boy liked his aunt so much, he had tried to get rid of the other two people in her life or at least turn her against them. Another consideration is whether he needed to shake up her comfortable world to make it more of a "home" for himself.

As noted, we try to follow up on cases to learn more about the accuracy of the 16PF test itself. Thus, we specifically asked Ms. M about her high scores on Self-Control (SC = 8.5) and her utter denial of tension and impatience (Q4 = 1). She explained the Self-Control in terms of a habit of tending to her corner of the bedroom while growing up. Unlike her siblings with whom she shared the room, she always kept her area and her belongings clean and orderly. To this day, she repeats this pattern by creating a comfortable, clean, and neat home in the midst of chaos. In regard to her low score on Tension (Q4), Ms. M laughed and said, "With my life? If I were the kind of person who got tense, I'd snap!"

CASE XIII: MR. N, AGE 47

REFERRAL

Mr. N called a therapist in private practice to seek help with long-standing dissatisfactions with his life. Although highly regarded at work, he reported not feeling as invested in it as he would like to be. His marriage of 13 years was successful by most measures (e.g., their two children were doing fine and each spouse treated the other well), but it was not a source of joy or even satisfaction. The 16PF Fifth Edition was administered after the first session to assist in treatment planning, and the Karson Clinical Report (KCR) was obtained and is reproduced following Mr. N's 16PF profile.

MR. N's 16PF Profile

Primary Traits

Factor		Sten
A	Warmth	4
B	Reasoning	10
C	Ego Strength	6
E	Assertiveness	3
F	Liveliness	5
G	Rule-Consciousness	4
H	Social Boldness	5
I	Sensitivity	5
L	Vigilance	2
M	Impracticality	8
N	Privateness	2
O	Apprehension	3
Q1	Openness to Change	9
Q2	Self-Reliance	5
Q3	Compulsivity	3
Q4	Tension	5

Response Set Scores

Scale		Percentile
IM	Impression Management	72
ACQ	Acquiescence	1
INF	Infrequency	51

Global Factors

Scale		Sten
EX	Extraversion	6.0
AX	Anxiety	3.0
TM	Tough-Mindedness	3.6
IN	Independence	4.2
SC	Self-Control	3.2

Karson Clinical Report (KCR) Narrative

Response Set Scores

The Infrequency index was within expected limits, indicating that Mr. N read the items carefully and understood what was required. Apparently, he did not present a particularly positive or negative impression of himself. Therefore, the information in this report is likely to be accurate.

Emotional Adjustment

Mr. N exhibits somewhat above-average ego strength, implying that response tendencies described in this report generally can be modulated or deferred to suit the occasion. Emotional stability is suggested as well as adequate frustration tolerance. His actual behavior in specific situations may not always reflect his underlying personality traits since he exhibits an ability to defer needs when necessary and to manage conflicting agendas. On the whole, his current above-average emotional adjustment seems to depend somewhat on his having found circumstances that do not overly challenge his defenses. Although his ego strength is adequate, he may not always possess a reliable degree of self-control in difficult situations. To maintain his positive emotional adjustment, he will need to keep formulating unique solutions to the demands made on him.

Interpersonal Issues

He is by no means socially isolated or withdrawn, but he does like to keep to himself more than many people do. If he cannot be alone when necessary, he may have to create personal space by distancing himself from others emotionally. He does not always put the time into relationships that is required. The fact that he is interpersonally reserved but also frank with others suggests that he may have little experience in groups or may naively expect others to value bluntness as he does.

Mr. N appears to be an unusually submissive and humble person, rarely taking active control of situations. He tends to experience things as happening to him, rather than as happening because of him. Others may neglect to take him into account in their plans as he does not always come across as someone to be reckoned with. His tendencies toward passivity can lead to an attitude of resentment toward people and events that he feels he cannot control.

He likes to say exactly what is on his mind with a bluntness and directness that sometimes can seem naive and indiscreet, and at other times, artless and disarming. In groups, for the sake of harmony and self-preservation, Mr. N may have to learn to curb his self-expression.

He is such a trusting, adaptable individual that sometimes others may take advantage of him. In other words, Mr. N rarely questions people's motives. Because he prefers to accommodate the needs of others, he may let them have their way just to avoid friction. Since others find this particular trait quite pleasant, Mr. N is usually perceived as likable. He appears to be about average on social boldness and group orientation. He is reasonably adept at crossing interpersonal distances and making contact with others, being about as much a team player as his peers.

SELF-CONTROL

Mr. N has little inclination to follow rules, and thus may lack one of the major motivations for doing what others expect. He is most likely to follow rules if they coincide with his own beliefs or agenda. Some of the tasks of living, usually taken for granted, may become optional in his mind. His energy level seems to be about average, suggesting that this is not a problem for him in general. He probably would not strike others as lacking in restraint or as being overly somber and serious.

He presents as a calm, self-assured individual, who does not often worry about getting into trouble and making mistakes. He may be on very good terms with his own conscience, which his below-average global Self-Control suggests is more carefree than approving.

Mr. N is not particularly organized or orderly. He does not always bother with details, and he may be too susceptible to the influence of recent events. In fact, he tends to make decisions before all the facts are known. Because of his relative paucity of good habits to rely on when necessary, he may be vulnerable to emotional distress.

COGNITION AND COMMUNICATION

He demonstrates superior abstract reasoning ability, with a capacity to understand complex ideas, to process complicated verbal material, and to grasp difficult concepts. For someone this intelligent not to be more assertive is somewhat unusual. Mr. N may lack confidence in the quality of his ideas. When he does express himself, his discomfort with the assertive role can make him blurt out whatever he is thinking, not always taking other people's reactions into account.

Mr. N is no more sensitive, thin-skinned, and tough-minded than most people. He does not neglect emotions, but neither is he inclined to sacrifice outcome for a smooth process. He is quite an imaginative and idea-oriented person who may be able to generate solutions that go beyond the needs of the immediate situation. However, Mr. N often fails to monitor the pragmatic consequences of ideas before embracing them. He may cling to impractical approaches longer than he should if they are appealing in theory. He sometimes ignores the exigencies of the stimulus situation confronting him. Consequently, attending to routine details is probably not his strong suit.

Mr. N reports being open to change to an unusual degree, actively seeking out novel experiences and new approaches. This implies flexibility, and does not necessarily mean he is ready to reject proven solutions just because they are not new. However, he may need to learn not to change course in some spheres just because doing so might be interesting.

FOLLOW-UP

The therapist gleaned from the KCR some of the main themes that the therapy would cover. These included Mr. N's excessive deference ($E = 3$, $L = 2$), his need for external structure ($G = 4$, $M = 8$, $Q3 = 3$, $SC = 3.2$), and his propensity for acting on impulses ($N = 2$, $O = 3$, $Q1 = 9$, $Q3 = 3$). His Reasoning ability ($B = 10$) and his Ego Strength ($C = 6$) were seen as holding the system together and as accounting for his accomplishments. Mr. N refused participation in group therapy to address his deference as well as in couple's therapy to explore his wife's role in complementing and possibly maintaining his deference, impulsivity, and reliance on external structure. Instead, he wanted his own therapy to work on these issues, and the therapist agreed to his terms. The therapy itself was considered a potential structural support in Mr. N's life and an ongoing relationship that could be used for interpreting instances of deferred aggression (which are bound to occur in any ongoing relationship) and for containing Mr. N's fantasy life to help him with his self-control. Eventually, the goal would be for the therapeutic dialogue to become internalized, to bolster Mr. N's intellect and will power in helping him integrate his various dynamics.

CASE XIV: MS. P, AGE 32

REFERRAL

Ms. P, a realtor, called a male therapist in private practice, seeking "psychoanalytic therapy." She mentioned the possibility of twice weekly sessions. The therapist suggested a two-hour initial consultation, administering the 16PF and scoring it by hand before meeting with her. (Scores on two of the validity scales— Acquiescence and Infrequency—are very time-consuming to score by hand and are not reported.)

MS. P's 16PF PROFILE

PRIMARY TRAITS

Factor		Sten
A	Warmth	8
B	Reasoning	7
C	Ego Strength	6
E	Assertiveness	7
F	Liveliness	8
G	Rule-Consciousness	7
H	Social Boldness	9
I	Sensitivity	3
L	Vigilance	5
M	Impracticality	5
N	Privateness	7
O	Apprehension	9
Q1	Openness to Change	8
Q2	Self-Reliance	6
Q3	Compulsivity	6
Q4	Tension	5

RESPONSE SET SCORES

Scale		Percentile
IM	Impression Management	72
ACQ	Acquiescence	Not reported
INF	Infrequency	Not reported

GLOBAL FACTORS

Scale		Sten
EX	Extraversion	7.1
AX	Anxiety	6.3
TM	Tough-Mindedness	5.2
IN	Independence	8.1
SC	Self-Control	5.9

PROFILE INTERPRETATION

With only a few minutes to absorb the scores before meeting with Ms. P, the therapist took note of the high score on Apprehension (O = 9) as the probable reason for referral. Although she may worry generally, the extent of her elevation on this scale suggested a situational exacerbation. This hypothesis was supported by signs of overall adjustment. For example, her global Anxiety score (AX = 6.3) would be average if her Apprehension score were only as high as 7. Her Extraversion (7.1) and Self-Control (5.9) scores suggested the presence of psychological resources. Finally, there were no other problem scores besides Apprehension.

The therapist noted her Independence (IN = 8.1) as a possible source of her worrying. Expression of Independence as anger is less likely in the warm (A = 8) interpersonal context suggested by her Extraversion and overall adjustment. Instead, it would likely be expressed as an adventurousness (Social Boldness [H = 9] and Openness to Change [Q1 = 8]) that get her into situations she feels guilty about.

Ms. P began the session by introducing herself as a relatively new mother of a 10-month-old boy and said that she had been married for 5 years to a successful manufacturer. She stated that a number of her friends had been in therapy and that she was interested in personal growth and self-exploration. The therapist could not help himself, and began to multiply his fee by two sessions per week, averaging 50 weeks a year. He said, "Gee, psychoanalytic therapy could cost you $40,000 if it lasted 5 years, perhaps even more." He continued, "I wonder what you could have done to think you need to pay that kind of penalty." The therapist's stance was based on his belief that his fantasizing about money said something about Ms. P.

Ms. P was a bit taken aback by his comment, and expressed her surprise. The therapist said, "Well, let me tell you what I think you would get for your $40,000. I think you would get to trust me deeply and completely. I'm not necessarily the most gifted therapist or the wisest. But I am truly trustworthy, and after years of meeting with me, you would come to realize this." The therapist continued, "So what I propose, if you're interested, is that we skip the five years, and just jump ahead to that moment when you truly trust me, when you tell me why you need this expiation."

Ms. P hemmed and hawed for several minutes. The therapist apologized for jumping to conclusions, suggesting she proceed telling about herself. Ms. P thought this over and blurted out that she had been involved in an affair with a young assistant professor at the university. They had met in the course of her work, when she was showing him houses. Taking advantage of their flexible work schedules, they had slept together several times. Eventually, she began to feel so guilty that she either had to tell her husband or break off the affair. She had chosen the latter course because she loved and respected her husband and wanted to continue making a life with him. She was seeking therapy to fix whatever was wrong with her, what had led to the affair.

The therapist questioned whether much was necessarily wrong with her. Ms. P admitted that the baby represented a terrible encroachment on her freedom and that she yearned for previous carefree, adventurous days. She said she may have panicked about becoming a mother, determined not to become her mother. This conversation about the situational determinants of the affair lasted through a second session. The therapist recommended that Ms. P stop trying to obtain absolution, since every time she told someone about the affair and every time she did an act of penance, it made things worse. Instead, the therapist suggested that Ms. P's penance should consist of carrying her guilty secret alone. The therapist said, "But if it's any consolation to you, I forgive you on behalf of all men everywhere, as long as you don't humiliate your husband by letting him find out and as long as you avoid the other guy like the plague." They agreed that if her attacks of guilt recurred and especially if she had an impulse to tell anyone else about the affair, she would call the therapist again.

FOLLOW-UP

Two months later, the therapist received a message on his answering machine from Ms. P. She reported having seen him in a local restaurant but not saying hello because she did not want to explain their acquaintance. "But I just had to call and thank you," she said. "You saved my life!" The therapist took the remark with a grain of salt, as an expression of Ms. P's Warmth (A) and Liveliness (F). The therapist also commented that he should have suggested a commission on the money he saved Ms. P.

Appendix A

Revisions of Personality Tests

Since its original publication in 1949, the 16PF has undergone four revisions, with the 16PF Fifth Edition being the most recent. A revision of the 16PF or any personality test typically is greeted by a natural reluctance on the part of clinicians. Subtle inferences may no longer apply to interpretations of the revised scales, and the research history of the test may not relate directly to the new version. The previous edition is better understood and better documented than the new test, and as a result, clinicians experienced in using the old test rightly have the most confidence in it.

Personality tests are not revised as a marketing ploy; rather, they are revised to ensure that they reflect contemporary language usage and relevant theoretical considerations. Tests also are revised to update their norms. The psychologist always has the responsibility to compare the individual client with a test's norm group to ascertain that it is relevant to the client. When too many years have passed since the norming of a test, no client can be represented confidently by the norm group.

At some point, the availability of the new edition and the applicability of its norms outweigh the familiarity of the previous edition, and the conversion is made. This frequently occurs first in forensic settings, where psychologists generally prefer defending the applicability of the research history to the revised test than the applicability of old norms to current clients. Therapists often are the last to convert since they usually do not have to defend their choice of instrument to anyone other than their clients or insurance companies (and old and new versions of tests normally cost about the same).

Appendix B

Forms of the 16PF

The 16PF is available in several different forms: the Fifth Edition, the Fourth Edition (Form A), and Forms A and B together. Each form has inherent advantages and disadvantages.

Our summary opinion about the Fifth Edition is that clinicians new to the 16PF, and even those who are moderately proficient with it, should use only the Fifth Edition. From the date of this book's publication, experts on Form A may justify waiting another year or so before using the Fifth Edition in any context other than direct work for clients. For the latter, we recommend a more extended transition, possibly over 3 or 4 years. Whenever an old version of the test is to be used, administering Forms A and B together is our preference because of thoroughness and enhanced reliability. However, we also recognize that the vast majority of 16PF administrations—even in highly contested forensic cases— involve only Form A, and this is clearly acceptable practice. (We do not advocate using Forms C, D, or E any longer in any setting, since, with the possible exception of Form E, their research history is not rich enough to recommend their usage over that of the Fifth Edition.)

Appendix C

Administration and Scoring of the 16PF

The clinician should take time to establish rapport with the client prior to administration of the 16PF. Perhaps the best operational definition of *rapport* is synonymous with Bordin's (1979) concept of the working alliance. For the 16PF, the alliance formed around answering the items honestly depends on a mutually defined and agreed upon goal, the relevance of the 16PF to attaining this goal, and the limited emotional bonds that can be established under the circumstances between clinician and client. In a therapeutic context, the goal often relates to the clinician's interest in understanding the client as well as possible. In other clinical contexts, the goal may concern returning to work, assisting counsel in preparing a defense, or regaining custody of children. A few words to the client about the purpose of personality testing may suffice to solidify the relevance of the 16PF to the goal. For example, the clinician might explain that thousands of people have answered the test's items and that a comparison between their responses and those of the client will reveal the client's personality traits. Often, what matters is not the rationale itself but the meta-communication of collaboration and mutuality that occurs when any rationale is offered. In a therapy setting, relating the 16PF to a goal is typically unnecessary since the client already understands the relevance of behavioral and trait-oriented questions to his or her reason for being there.

Obviously, deep emotional bonds do not develop between a clinician and client during a psychological evaluation; however, steps can be taken to optimize the emotional rapport. These typically relate to the structure of the relationship. Communicating respect by honoring time commitments, being prepared, and apologizing for any inconveniences will help maintain most social relationships and can occasion a spirit of cooperation in the testing enterprise as well.

The setting for administration of the 16PF should be a comfortable, quiet, well-ventilated, and properly lighted room. Accommodating the client in this manner not only relates to courtesy but also to reproducing the administration conditions under which the test was normed.

Both the test's directions and items are written at the fifth-grade level. The clinician may read the directions aloud or have the client read them silently. A client suspected as being unable to read at the fifth-grade level should be requested to read the directions aloud. The directions emphasize that the client should give the first natural response that occurs to him or her, and we reiterate this instruction orally at the start of testing. Most clients finish the 16PF Fifth Edition within 35 to 50 minutes. A client on a pace to exceed the 50-minute completion time should be reminded to give the first natural response.

IPAT, publisher of the 16PF, offers the 16PF Fifth Edition via OnSite System software, which enables the client to take the test on an IBM or IBM-compatible personal computer. This method of administration accelerates not only the testing time but also the scoring process. Of course, this option requires that both the clinician and client are comfortable with using a computer and that a terminal is available in an appropriate setting.

Most 16PF testings are done with pencil and answer sheet. The answer sheet may be hand- or computer-scored. If the answer sheet is to be computer-scored, all the grids on the left-hand side of the answer sheet must be completed, although an ID number may be substituted for the client's name if confidentiality is desired. At the conclusion of testing and regardless of the scoring method to be used, the clinician must review the answer sheet to ensure that all items have been answered. For missing responses to Reasoning (B) items, the client should be encouraged to guess. Any multiple responses to items should be reduced to a single choice. Sometimes reviewing the answer sheet before the client leaves is not feasible, and sometimes clients refuse to answer every item. In these circumstances, extrapolating raw scores on factors with omissions is permissible as long as the unanswered items do not exceed 12 on the whole test. Thirteen or more omissions will invalidate the test (Russell & Karol, 1994, p. 9).

Three of the 16PF scales—Warmth (A), Assertiveness (E), and Sensitivity (I)—can be scored with either combined-sex or sex-specific norms. We recommend sex-specific norms for all clinical applications.

Detailed instructions for scoring the test are presented in *The 16PF Fifth Edition Administrator's Manual* (Russell & Karol, 1994, pp. 7-13). For handscoring, templates from IPAT must be used to obtain raw scores on the 16 primary factors and the Impression Management (IM) index. No templates are available for scoring the Infrequency (INF) and Acquiescence (ACQ) indices. For most clinical purposes, it is usually sufficient to scan the answer sheet for excessive use of the *a, b,* or *c* response alternatives or for any unusual response pattern. When INF and ACQ raw scores are needed, they can be obtained by a laborious process that involves looking up the items listed for each scale (Russell & Karol, 1994, p. 138 and p. 140). Raw scores are converted to sten scores by use of a table (Russell & Karol, 1994, p. 133). If desired, global scores can be computed with the aid of a profile sheet available from IPAT. The primary and global scores can be plotted on the profile sheet to assist the clinician in visualizing the scores.

For computer-scoring, certain requirements must be met depending on the choice of methods. These can be obtained from IPAT. The OnSite System scores the test automatically. The OnFax System reads a faxed answer sheet and then faxes back the scores and a selected computerized interpretive report. Answer sheets also can be mailed to IPAT for computer-scoring.

APPENDIX D

THE KARSON CLINICAL REPORT (KCR)

Clinicians may want to consider obtaining the Karson Clinical Report (KCR), which is available from IPAT, publisher of the 16PF. We wrote a computerized interpretive report because many clinicians are unaware of all the relevant inferences that the 16PF can provide. The computer program that produces the KCR mimics our approach to interpreting the various scales. Our goal was to produce a readable, useful report that bridges the gap between the test scores and the user's needs.

Ideally, the KCR is like having a consultation with us, albeit only on the basis of the 16PF scores. The report does not integrate its inferences with special circumstances, life history, precipitating events, and referral questions. Therefore, the clinician must integrate the reported information into the comprehensive assessment process. That integration is facilitated by many of the statements included in the KCR narrative. Aspects of the KCR can be discussed openly with clients; however, because the KCR requires a clinician's judgment, it should not be shared directly with the client.

NOTES

CHAPTER 2: GENERAL INTERPRETIVE CONSIDERATIONS

1. Originally, problem scores were derived for the 16PF Fourth Edition. On two separate occasions, one of us (S. K.) was interviewed concerning which scores on any scales "in and of themselves imply psychopathology or adjustment problems." Then the problem scores were validated in industrial settings by their ability to distinguish successful from poorly rated employees across several different job types. (Certain problem scores might not differentiate between levels of performance on some jobs, but in our experience, no problem score has ever been associated with job success.) For the 16PF Fifth Edition, the list of problem scores was tailored based on clinical judgment and analysis of a sample of 250 protocols of clients who took both the 16PF Fourth Edition and the 16PF Fifth Edition.

CHAPTER 3: THE CONSTRUCTION OF THE 16PF

1. These 5 bipolar factors are extraversion, neuroticism, control, aggression, and (depending on the theorist) refinement or femininity or openness to experience. Different theorists also assign varying names to the first 4 factors, but all seemingly describe the same concepts. The 5 factors are very similar to the 16PF's global factors of Extraversion, Anxiety, Tough-Mindedness, Independence, and Self-Control. Our approach to interpreting the 16PF, regardless of the theoretical debates on the optimal number of factors, is that 5 factors are too few for clinical purposes. Cattell (Cattell & Krug, 1986) believes that 16 factors are required (the derivation of the 16PF name) and that using only 5 loses too much information.

CHAPTER 4: THE SCALES OF THE 16PF

1. An important distinction between the strategies for writing items for Form A and for the Fifth Edition affects the interpretations of certain scales from one test to the other. Items on the affected Form A scales address the expression of the source trait in a variety of situations. The items are not highly correlated with one another, and in some instances, are not highly correlated with the factor they purport to measure. This occurred because the situations evoked by the items were complex enough to tap other traits.

The affected Fifth Edition scales contain items that are highly correlated with each other and with the factor. This was achieved by simplifying the items and making them alike. As a result, many of the scales have much greater face validity and improved reliabilities than their Form A counterparts.

Each approach to item writing has its merits and disadvantages. The merits of validity and reliability are well known to psychologists, but as Cattell et al. (1970, p. 32) pointed out:

> If one wishes to create high homogeneities (and call them reliabilities!) as some test handbooks do, it is easily possible to do so by multiplying the writing of very similar items. But any broad and important personality trait has to be assessed across a wide variety of areas and forms of expression. Furthermore, even from a purely psychometric point of view, the highest multiple-R validity is obtained by finding items which correlate consistently with the factor, but trivially with one another.

2. Two sources of unpublished information on which we have based many of our comments about 16PF interpretations may be of particular interest.

The first concerns an effort by us (J. O. and S. K.) to discover how one clinician actually uses the 16PF factor scores in clinical situations (in contrast to the many interpretive programs and books that are modeled on how senior clinicians "think" they use the data). J. O. objectively evaluated about 100 blind interpretations done by S. K. to determine how S. K. translated specific factor scores into descriptive language. Interpretive reports were analyzed factor by factor, and each sentence or phrase linked to a specific factor score was isolated. These distilled interpretations of different scores form the basis for many of our ideas about the factors presented in this chapter.

The second source of information on which many of our interpretations rely is an analysis of 250 protocols of clients who took both Form A and the Fifth Edition. Regression analyses of the established scales against each new scale helped shape our sense of the new factors. Further, each Form A protocol was subjected to algorithms developed from thousands of industrial uses of the 16PF to divide the pool into two groups analogous to probable hires or promotions and probable nonhires or nonpromotions. Obviously, personality testing is only one source of information in actual personnel decision-making, but the algorithms developed at work sites seemed appropriate for distinguishing potentially problematic functioning in a nonclinical sample. While certain features of the 16PF naturally vary in desirability depending on the particular job, we found that other features are associated with successful performance regardless of the type of job. These latter features involve overall mental health issues, and were used to distinguish two groups that we called "Pass" and "Fail." Each 16PF Fifth Edition scale was evaluated with respect to its distribution between these two groups; this was essential to our applying the concept of problem scores to the Fifth Edition.

3. Uncited statements about relationships between 16PF factors and jobs are based on over 10,000 industrial 16PF uses and 15 unpublished studies of successful versus unsuccessful performance in various occupations ranging from bank personnel to security guards to sales.

4. A mild caution in regard to interpreting the Fifth Edition's Warmth (A) scale involves clients with an idiosyncratic experience of architecture. Those with a fondness for architecture may score lower on Factor A than they should, for 2 of the scale's 11 items mention architects as examples of low Warmth (A-) types. Any item on any test can generate measurement error as a result of an idiosyncratic response from a client, but repeating terms on short scales incurs extra risk.

5. The distinction between assertiveness and dominance is worth documenting. On the Form A items linked to dominance, high scorers have to acknowledge *being critical, forceful, sarcastic, commanding,* and *superior;* on the Fifth Edition items, high scorers have to acknowledge less powerful descriptors such as *assertive, pointing out mistakes,* or *complaining about bad service.* The Fifth Edition version of Factor E (assertiveness) and the Form A version of Factor E (dominance) correlate differently with certain Form A factors, all in the direction that would support the new interpretation of assertiveness. Assertiveness (Fifth Edition) versus dominance (Form A) is more related to the Form A version of ego strength ($r = .21$ vs. $-.09$), less related to unconventionality ($r = .03$ vs. $-.27$), less related to suspiciousness ($r = .11$ vs. $.38$), more related to groundedness ($r = .06$ vs. $.40$), more related to calmness ($r = -.29$ vs. $-.09$), and less related to disorderliness ($r = -.04$ vs. $-.23$) (Conn & Rieke, 1994, p. 97 compared with Cattell et al., 1970, p. 113). Using the Fifth Edition as a "yardstick" to distinguish the two scales, we found that assertiveness (Fifth Edition) versus dominance (Form A) is less related to unconventionality ($r = -.06$ vs. $-.30$), less related to impracticality ($r = -.02$ vs. $.16$), more related to forthrightness ($r = -.12$ vs. $-.29$), and less related to disorderliness ($r = .10$ vs. $-.13$)(Conn & Rieke, 1994, p. 94 compared with p. 97).

6. S. Karson and J. W. O'Dell developed an unpublished, cross-validated depression scale for Form A on a carefully diagnosed sample of dysthymic reactions in the U.S. Foreign Service.

7. Factor L does not typically correlate with MMPI's 6-Pa scale (Karson & O'Dell, 1987). This is not surprising since Pa is composed of both persecutory and naive subscales. Further, MMPIers suggest interpreting both high scores and very low scores on Pa as indicative of paranoia, a possibility we have raised for Factor L as well.

Chapter 5: Response Set or Validity Scales

1. The Institute for Personality and Ability Testing, Inc. (IPAT), publisher of the 16PF Fifth Edition, provided us with data on 5,269 individuals. With so many subjects, correlations with an absolute value greater than .08 are significant at the .01 level, but are hardly meaningful clinically. Traits mentioned in the text

associate with the Acquiescence (ACQ) scale have correlations with an absolute value greater than .20. To ensure that the pattern of traits reported in the text is not an artifact of test construction, one must compare the factors that correlate with the ACQ scale with the pattern that emerges when a subject merely selects the *a* alternative to all test items. In other words, because the *true* alternative is always the *a* alternative, one can infer that the ACQ scale measures the tendency to agree with all item stems only if it does not merely measure the tendency to answer *a* to all items. However, a pattern of all *a* responses will produce only a few factor sten scores outside the average range of 5 to 6, and these do not include the key ACQ-associated factors of Assertiveness (E), Social Boldness (H), and Vigilance (L). Therefore, subjects scoring high on ACQ would seem to be indiscriminately agreeing with item stems rather than indiscriminately choosing the *a* response alternative.

CHAPTER 6: GLOBAL FACTORS

1. An analogy may be illustrative. On the WISC-R, factor analyses yielded a Freedom from Distractibility factor, involving scaled scores on Arithmetic, Coding, and Digit Span. This factor was useful in detecting attention deficit disorder, and indeed a good correspondence existed between the subtests associated with ADD-H identified by clinical and research data and those lumped together by the factor analyses. With the WISC-III's inclusion of Symbol Search, however, an additional factor emerged, which researchers named Processing Speed. Coding scores load much more heavily on the new factor than on the old. A complete correspondence no longer exists between the mathematically derived factor called Freedom from Distractibility and the clinically relevant one, but the clinician cannot ignore Coding in trying to detect attention deficits.

2. Krug and Johns (1986) credit Karson and Pool (1958) as being among the first to identify and replicate this factor.

References

Allport, G. W., & Odbert, H. S. (1936). Trait-names: A psycholexical study. *Psychological Monographs, 47.*

Bordin, E. S. (1979). The generalizability of the psychoanalytic concept of the working alliance. *Psychotherapy: Theory, Research, and Practice, 16*(3), 252-260.

Cattell, H. B. (1989). *The 16PF: Personality in depth.* Champaign, IL: Institute for Personality and Ability Testing, Inc.

Cattell, R. B. (1936). Temperament tests in clinical practice. *British Journal of Medical Psychology, 16,* 43-61.

Cattell, R. B. (1943). The description of personality: Basic traits resolved into clusters. *Journal of Abnormal and Social Psychology, 38,* 476-506.

Cattell, R. B. (1946). *The description and measurement of personality.* New York: Harcourt, Brace & World.

Cattell, R. B. (1950). *Personality, a systematic theoretical and factual study.* New York: McGraw-Hill.

Cattell, R. B. (1957). *Personality and motivation structure and measurement.* New York: World Book.

Cattell, R. B. (1973). *Personality and mood by questionnaire.* San Francisco: Jossey-Bass.

Cattell, R. B. (1976). Foreword. In S. Karson & J. W. O'Dell, *A guide to the clinical use of the 16PF.* Champaign, IL: Institute for Personality and Ability Testing, Inc.

Cattell, R. B. (1994). Constancy of global, second-order personality factors over a twenty-year-plus period. *Psychological Reports, 75,* 3-9.

Cattell, R. B., Eber, H. W., & Tatsuoka, M. M. (1970). *Handbook for the Sixteen Personality Factor Questionnaire (16PF).* Champaign, IL: Institute for Personality and Ability Testing, Inc.

Cattell, R. B., & Krug, S. E. (1986). The number of factors in the 16PF: A review of the evidence with special emphasis on methodological problems. *Educational and Psychological Measurement, 46,* 509-520.

Conn, S. R., & Rieke, M. L. (Eds.). (1994). *16PF Fifth Edition technical manual.* Champaign, IL: Institute for Personality and Ability Testing, Inc.

Dana, R., Bolton, B., & Gritzmacher, S. (1983). 16PF source traits associated with DSM-III symptoms for four diagnostic groups. *Journal of Clinical Psychology, 39,* 958-960.

Dana, R., Bolton, B., & West, V. (1983). Validation of eisegesis concepts in assessment reports using the 16PF: A training method with examples. *Proceedings of the Third International Conference on the 16PF* (pp. 20-29). Champaign, IL: Institute for Personality and Ability Testing, Inc.

Deutsch, H. (1942). Some forms of emotional disturbance and their relationship to schizophrenia. *Psychoanalytic Quarterly, 11,* 301-321.

Endres, L. S., Guastello, S. J., & Rieke, M. L. (1992). Meta-interpretive reliability of computer-based test interpretations: The Karson Clinical Report. *Journal of Personality Assessment, 59,* 448-467.

Gerbing, D. W., & Tuley, M. R. (1991). The 16PF related to the five-factor model of personality: Multiple-indicator measurement versus the a priori scales. *Multivariate Behavioral Research, 26,* 271-289.

Goldberg, L. R. (1993). The structure of phenotypic personality traits. *American Psychologist, 48,* 26-34.

Golden, C. J. (1990). *Clinical interpretation of objective psychological tests* (2nd ed.). Needham Heights, MA: Allyn and Bacon.

Herman, K., & Usita, P. (1994). Predicting Big Brothers/Big Sisters volunteer attrition with the 16PF. *Child and Youth Care Forum, 23,* 207-211.

Horney, K. (1950). *Neurosis and human growth.* New York: Norton.

Jacobson, E. (1971). *Depression: Comparative studies of normal, neurotic and psychotic conditions.* New York: International Universities Press.

Karson, M. (1980). Is aesthetic judgment impaired by neuroticism? *Journal of Personality Assessment, 44,* 499-506.

Karson, S. (1960). Validating clinical judgments with the 16PF test. *Journal of Clinical Psychology, 16,* 394-397.

Karson, S., & Karson, M. (1995). *The 16PF Fifth Edition Karson Clinical Report manual.* Champaign, IL: Institute for Personality and Ability Testing, Inc.

Karson, S., & O'Dell, J. W. (1974). Personality makeup of the American air traffic controller. *Aerospace Medicine, 45,* 1001-1007.

Karson, S., & O'Dell, J. W. (1976). *A guide to the clinical use of the 16PF.* Champaign, IL: Institute for Personality and Ability Testing, Inc.

Karson, S., & O'Dell, J. W. (1987). Personality profiles in the U.S. foreign service. In J. N. Butcher & C. D. Spielberger (Eds.), *Advances in personality assessment* (Vol. VI). Hillsdale, NJ: Lawrence Erlbaum Associates.

Karson, S., & O'Dell, J. W. (1987a). Computer-based interpretation of the 16PF: The Karson Clinical Report in contemporary practice. In J. N. Butcher (Ed.), *Computerized psychological assessment: A practitioner's guide.* New York: Basic Books.

Karson, S., & O'Dell, J. W. (1989). The 16PF. In C. S. Newmark (Ed.), *Major psychological assessment instruments* (Vol. II). Needham Heights, MA: Allyn and Bacon.

Karson, S., & Pool, K. (1958). Second-order factors in personality measurement. *Journal of Consulting Psychology, 23,* 299-303.

Katz, J. (1973). *Validity of self-appraisals of mental health.* Unpublished doctoral dissertation, The University of Michigan, Ann Arbor.

Kernberg, O. (1975). *Borderline conditions and pathological narcissism.* New York: Jason Aronson.

Kernberg, O. (1984). *Severe personality disorders.* New Haven, CT: Yale University Press.

Kleinmutz, B. (1982). *Personality and psychological assessment.* New York: St. Martin's Press.

Kline, P. (1993). *Handbook of psychological testing.* New York: Rutledge.

Krug, S. E. (Ed.). (1977). *Psychological assessment in medicine.* Champaign, IL: Institute for Personality and Ability Testing, Inc.

Krug, S. E. (1981). *Interpreting 16PF profile patterns.* Champaign, IL: Institute for Personality and Ability Testing, Inc.

Krug, S. E. (1994). Personality: A Cattellian perspective. In S. Strack & M. Lorr (Eds.), *Differentiating normal and abnormal personality.* New York: Springer.

Krug, S. E., & Johns, E. F. (1986). A large scale cross validation of second-order personality structure defined by the 16PF. *Psychological Reports, 59,* 683-693.

Maslow, A. (1968). *Toward a psychology of being* (2nd ed.). Princeton, NJ: Insight Books.

Melamed, T. (1992). Personality correlates of physical height. *Personality and Individual Differences, 13,* 1349-1350.

Mershon, B., & Gorsuch, R. L. (1988). Number of factors in the personality sphere. *Journal of Personality and Social Psychology, 55,* 675-680.

Meyer, R. G. (1993). *The clinician's handbook* (3rd ed.). Needham Heights, MA: Allyn and Bacon.

Moreland, K. L. (1985). Validation of computer-based test interpretation: Problems and prospects. *Journal of Consulting and Clinical Psychology, 55,* 113-114.

Murphy, K. R. (1987). The accuracy of clinical versus computerized test interpretations. *American Psychologist, 42,* 192-193.

Nietzsche, F. (1966). Beyond good and evil. In W. Kaufmann (Ed. and Trans.), *Basic writings of Nietzsche.* New York: Modern Library. (Original work published 1886)

O'Dell, J. W., & Karson, S. (1969). Some relationships between the MMPI and 16PF. *Journal of Clinical Psychology, 25*(3), 279-283.

Rahe, R., Karson, S., Howard, N., Rubin, R. T., & Poland, R. E. (1990). Psychological and physiological assessments on American hostages freed from captivity in Iran. *Psychosomatic Medicine, 52,* 1-16.

Russell, M. T., & Karol, D. L. (1994). *The 16PF Fifth Edition administrator's manual.* Champaign, IL: Institute for Personality and Ability Testing, Inc.

Shedler, J., Mayman, M., & Manis, M. (1993). The illusion of mental health. *American Psychologist, 48,* 1117-1131.

Skinner, B. F. (1953). *Science and human behavior.* New York: The Free Press.

Watkins, C. E., Jr., Campbell, V. L., Nieberding, R., & Hallmark, R. (1995). Contemporary practice of psychological assessment by clinical psychologists. *Professional Psychology: Research and Practice, 26,* 54-60.